JOHN JAMES BEZER
Chartist

AND

JOHN ARNOTT
General Secretary,
National Charter Association

by DAVID SHAW

CONTENTS

JOHN JAMES BEZER, CHARTIST

JOHN ARNOTT, NATIONAL CHARTER ASSOCIATION

LIST OF ILLUSTRATIONS

Fleet Street c. 1830

The view is taken beyond Fetter Lane on the right. Temple Bar is in the background. Showing the clock of St Dunstan in the West, with Clark and Wetherly, goldsmiths. Thomas Redshaw bookseller is at No. 186, and Edward Cane ironmonger at No, 185. John James Bezer's bookshop at the Society for Promoting Working Men's Associations, No. 183, would have been between No. 185 and Fetter Lane which is not covered by the view. See page 47.

JOHN JAMES BEZER
1816 - 1888
CHARTIST

INTRODUCTION

"It is said, God made everything. I don't believe it; He never made Whitecross Place, the entrance to which was the narrow way that leadeth into stinks. A gutter passed through the middle of the court - a pretty looking gutter, from which the effluvia rose up, without ceasing, into our elegant second floor front; a room, or rather a cell (we paid 2s. 3d. rent weekly, for the blessed privilege of breathing in the accumulated filth below); a hole in which the bugs held a monster public meeting every night, determined to show what a co-operative movement could do."
JOHN JAMES BEZER.

JOHN JAMES BEZER was a minor but interesting activist during the later years of the Chartist movement. His name comes down to us, not so much by way of references made to his lectures and the Chartist meetings that he attended in company with the movement's more notable personalities, but through the record of his trial for sedition and, more particularly, for his incomplete autobiography. Ten chapters of this were published as installments in the *Christian Socialist*, from 9 August 1851. Bezer's narrative of his childhood and early days provide an important and incisive account of the wretched lives suffered by London's poor during the early 1800's. He probably intended to cover the period of his trial and subsequent incarceration in Newgate Prison, but his autobiography ceased with the demise of the *Christian Socialist* in 1851, and Bezer left the Chartist scene in 1852. Although written anonymously, from reading the *Christian Socialist* it is not difficult to determine him as being the author.

There is little information regarding his early personal activities other than those given in his autobiography. However, there are reports of his rather short-lived political pursuits in radical newspapers, as well as items in the *Christian Socialist*. From information that has been obtained, including genealogical records that have been traced, a chronological order has been used. Further information may yet become available. From these records, it is surprising to note how many times he and his family moved, usually within the Clerkenwell, Shoreditch, and Bethnal Green areas. He mentioned in a letter to the *Christian Socialist* (see the section 'Circulation of the *Christian Socialist*') that he had had nine children up to December 1851 - but details of only eight have been traced. Probably the other child died at an early age, and that record has so far not been found.

An autodidact as were many of the poorer class at that time - see, for example, Gerald Massey - he was clever, observant, a practical opportunist and had a descriptive dry sense of humour. His early involvement with the Chartist movement certainly provided a positive outlet for his rebellious opinions, the result of his experience of poverty and social injustice. Undoubtedly sincere, his active participation within the Chartist organisation and Christian Socialist movement was essentially localised and he was politically well informed, but he showed little evidence of any wide knowledge of political complexities. Neither did he appear to show any desire for gaining personal achievement through concentration of purpose, as his very varied occupations show.

With regard to his personal appearance, he was blind in his left eye, the result of smallpox as a child and, confirmed from later information, was of very short stature at only 5 feet high. In his autobiography he mentioned [about 1835] that he had been advised to give up shoemaking, as it was straining his eye, but according to records, he continued with the occupation at intervals for a number of years.

The sources used for both John James Bezer and John Arnott remain textually accurate, though some alterations have been made to the original formats in order to make for greater ease of reading in this presentation. All necessary references are given either in the text, or following each particular section.

PART ONE.

1.

Destitution and Intrigues

John James Bezer was born on the 24 August 1816 in his father's one room barber's shop in Hope Street, Spitalfields, and baptised on the 15 September 1816 at Spitalfields Christ Church, Stepney.

The Hope Street map area (see illustration) is dated 1813, and the street - now redeveloped - is situated in the area today between Brick Lane, Quaker Street and Grey Eagle Street.

Hope Street, 1813

His father was a drunkard and spendthrift, and the family became out-door paupers, the parish allowing them four shillings per week. At nine years of age, young Bezer obtained his first post as a warehouse errand boy in Newgate Street. Working a 17-hour day for a six-day week, he received three shillings. At one time, he and his mother lived in Whitecross Place, near the Barbican, about which he said:

"It is said, God made everything. I don't believe it; He never made Whitecross Place, the entrance to which was the narrow way that leadeth into stinks. A gutter passed through the middle of the court - a pretty looking gutter, from which the effluvia rose up, without ceasing, into our elegant second floor front; a room, or rather a cell (we paid 2s. 3d. rent weekly, for the blessed privilege of breathing in the accumulated filth below); a hole in which the bugs held a monster public meeting every night, determined to show what a co-operative movement could do."

Whitecross Place - "the place of stinks" is illustrated from the 1813 map beneath Crown Street. It shows the narrow entrance (Whitecross Alley) from Wilson Street, at the South-east of Finsbury Square leading into an irregular enclosed area. Although some improvements had been made since that time, Charles Booth noted it in his 1898 poverty map as belonging to the lowest, very poor class. It is still marked on maps today, at the corner of Wilson Street and Sun Street.

Whitecross Place, 1813

Between January and July 1837 (records destroyed during the war), he married Jane Sarah Drew at Christchurch Newgate Street, and the birth of their first child occurred the following year. Francis James Bezer was born at 6 am on 6 February 1838 at 30, Back Hill, Saffron Hill.

Bezer was listed then as a 'Town Traveller', a broad term, for at that time he was jobless, and reduced to singing hymns and begging.

The map illustrated, (1816) shows Back Hill to the north of Leather Lane.

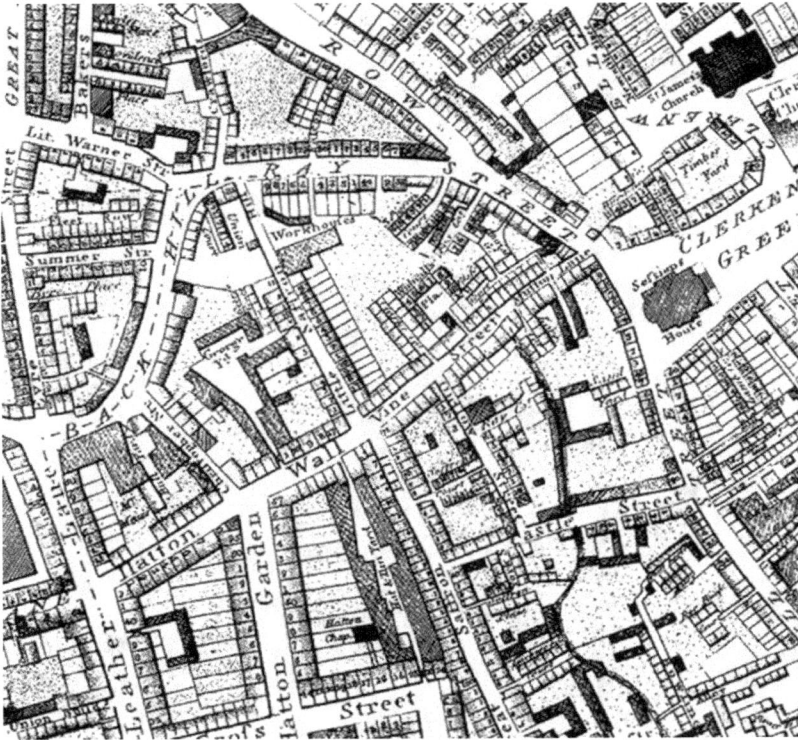

Back Hill, 1816

The couple's second child, Jane Sarah Bezer was born on 24 September 1839 at 33 St Helena Place, Clerkenwell. Bezer listed as a 'labourer.' St Helena Place was between Farringdon Road and Aldersgate Street. It is unmarked on current maps, but was mentioned in Charles Booth's 1898 notes as then being rough, doors open, windows broken, women wearing sackcloth instead of skirts. Unfortunately, little Jane did not survive long, having been found dead in bed on the 12 December

1839 (Informant: the Coroner). There was no evidence to prove the cause of death. Bezer is listed as a 'Shoemaker.'

A third child, Jane Mary Bezer was born on 26 September 1840 at 2 Baldwin's Place, Baldwin's Gardens, Holborn. Bezer listed again as a Shoe Maker. Baldwin's Place was situated off Gray's Inn Road between what is now Baldwin's Gardens and Portpool Lane. Charles Booth's later 1898 notes refer to the area as dull, messy, with airless courts. The children pale, but fairly well dressed and clean.

Ray Street, Clerkenwell (about 1820), showing part of Ray Street (left, which continues to Back Hill), with St James' Church in the background. The cattle would be on their way to Smithfield. Ray Street is marked on maps today, but is crossed by the Farringdon Road, and the surroundings changed by increased redevelopment.

In 1841, the census return shows the family still living in Baldwin's Place, St Andrew above the Bar. Bezer is listed as aged 25, a Journeyman Shoemaker with his wife 25, a Dressmaker, and Jane Bezer, 9 months. Her son, Francis James, is not listed at that time.

About 1842, in common with many other workers who were suffering social iniquity, Bezer joined the Chartist movement, soon becoming Secretary of the Cripplegate Locality of the National Charter Association, and speaking at their meetings.

Bezer's next child was Emily Drew Bezer, born on 20 May 1843, at 4 Carr Square, St Giles Cripplegate. Bezer is listed as a 'Cordwainer' [a shoe or boot maker]. Carr Square was west of Moor Lane – now redeveloped, and near Moorgate tube station.

Another son followed fairly quickly, as did another move:

Frederick John Bezer was born on 1 December 1844 at 7 Hanover Court, St Giles Cripplegate. Bezer remained listed as a Cordwainer. Hanover Court was between Milton Street and Moor Lane, and the area is redeveloped. The site would be approximately, where Milton Court is today.

Another daughter, Mary Nelson Bezer was born on 4 August 1846. The family had moved yet again, this time to 5 Bromleys Buildings, Bread Street Hill. Bezer now listed as a 'General Dealer'. Bromleys Buildings were between Huggin Lane and Bread Street Hill. Bread Street Hill is now the area of Bread Street between Queen Victoria Street and Cannon Street, near Mansion House tube station.

Bezer's third son was next on the scene. Walter Cooper Bezer was born on 10 July 1848, at 2, Shepherd and Flock Court, Little Bell Alley, North East of the City of London. Bezer listed now as a 'Fishmonger', the occupation he gave when he was arrested the following month. Shepherd and Flock Court was situated off White Alley, Coleman Street (near the Bank of England), and between Little Bell Alley that ran between the east end of Great Bell Alley and London Wall. The area was rebuilt c. 1890. There is a short stretch of Great Bell Alley off Coleman Street that is still marked on maps today, south of Moorgate tube station. The name of 'Walter Cooper' may have been given as an association with Walter Cooper who became Manager in 1850 of the Working Tailor's Association, Castle Street. Cooper had been lecturing prior to this, Gerald Massey having come into contact with him in 1849.

In 1848, following the failure of the Kennington Common rally on the 10 April and the petition to Parliament, a number of militant Chartists convened private meetings with the object "if possible, to destroy the power of the Queen, and establish a Republic." All these meetings were undertaken apparently without the knowledge of the Executive of the National Charter Association. Bezer gave covert assistance, and was able to inform those members involved that he - amongst others - would be able to supply 50 fighting men, and that they 'were going to get up a bloody revolution'. However, Government spies defeated the plan; six of the plotters were transported to Australia, and fifteen imprisoned (*The Times*, 23 September 1848).

Shortly after the Kennington Common episode, and following an address he gave at a public meeting [see Regina v. Bezer], Bezer was convicted of sedition [inciting resistance to lawful authority and tending to cause the disruption or overthrow of the government. Ed.] and sentenced to two years imprisonment in London's notorious Newgate prison.

Prior to his arrest in 1848, he had been on the Committee and was an active member of the Irish Democratic Confederation of London - a strongly militant group that had Feargus O'Connor as president. The objectives of this Confederation included the repeal of the Union between Great Britain and Ireland and the establishment of a representative parliament. Bezer had lectured on the Irish question as well as on Chartist themes at various venues throughout the previous twelve months, including Cartwright's Coffee House, Cripplegate; the Star Coffee House Redcross Street, Golden Lane, and the Literary and Scientific Institution, John Street, Fitzroy Square.

A public meeting complaining of police action against Chartists was held at the latter venue on the 22 June, 1848. At this meeting, Bezer moved 'That making the police a military body was subversive of liberty, and the British Constitution.' (*Northern Star*, 1 July, 1848.)

That year was ending most unkindly for Bezer. His son, Frederick John Bezer, then aged nearly four years, caught Scarlet Fever in the early part of August. Unfortunately, it was the malignant type, and the child died of 'cerebral effusion' on the 1 September, soon after Bezer entered Newgate prison. His wife was now residing at 3 Sherroll's Buildings, St. Botolph, Bishopsgate. The address has not been identified on available maps.

2.

REGINA *v.* BEZER 1848

THE TRIAL OF JOHN JAMES BEZER FOR SEDITION.

BACKGROUND

On the 26 July 1848 Bezer was with John Shaw at the City Lecture Theatre, Milton Street, Cripplegate, where the subject was 'Of bringing before the Legislature and the Public the despotic treatment of the Chartist victims.' A strong force of police was standing by in case of disturbance. Two days later - at the same venue - Bezer was again with John Shaw who was conducting a public meeting condemning the Government's handling of the current problems in Ireland. It was reported that some 1,000 persons mostly Irish were in attendance both inside and outside the hall. Also present were the police and reporters who busied themselves by taking notes of the meeting that had been advertised as 'Is Ireland Up?'

Consequently, John Shaw, the meeting's Chairman and Bezer, together with four others were indicted for sedition.

Bezer's trial came up at the Central Criminal Court in August where, in the indictment, he was referred to as being a "wicked, malicious, seditious and evil disposed person."

TRIAL

The Attorney-General opened the case and read the defendant's "false, seditious and inflammatory words and matter" in transcript:

'Now then, to the Resolution I hold in my hand. Resolved that this Meeting deeply sympathise with the struggling people of Ireland, and is resolved to assist them by all and every means in their power, and that we consider the physical preparations of the Government unjustifiable without the proper remedial measures attached thereto.

Brother Chartists, Brother Republicans, Brother Democrats, for I don't know that I can address you by any better name than Democrats, for the principle of Democracy is the principle of a free stage to all and no favour to any. The principle of Democracy is the right of the rich and no more. The principle of Democracy is the right of the poor and no less. The principle of Democracy is the greatest amount of good to the greatest number. In short, the principle of Democracy is the principle of Justice and of truth. Democrats understand each other all over the world. Democrats are the same in every nation. The Democrats of Russia, the Democrats of Poland, the Democrats of Switzerland, the Democrats of Germany, the Democrats of France, the Democrats of Ireland understand each other. They are all travelling the same road; they have all one end; they have all one aim; they have all one object in view and that object is glorious liberty. They are all singing one song - not in the same language perhaps, but the same sentiment:

> 'Oh Liberty when will man resign thee
> Once having felt thy generous flame;
> Or whips thy noble spirit tame.'
> Shall locks or bolts or bars confine thee

No! It has not tamed John Mitchell yet, I will be bound. It has not yet tamed Ernest Jones I will be bound. Did it tame the men of old when they were burned at the stake? No, it did not. It actually progressed their principles more than they would have progressed - and let Tyrants beware - you had better shut up shop - you had better put up your swords and cut and run, for democracy is spreading. Depend upon it. And sooner or later will overwhelm you all.

My friends, we live in strange times; we live in very queer times and yet it is a privilege to live in these times. We have seen a great many things. We have seen Lords and Dukes and Princes and all the rest of the mob in different nations cut and run. Louis Phillipe had to change his clothes and his whiskers and to take his umbrella and run and cut away. We have seen great changes and we shall live to see greater changes yet. As a Democrat I hope so, and as I said before, I don't know that I can address you by any better word than Democrats.

I might say, Mr Chairman and all respectable people, and for this reason, because every man that works for his living honestly either by his head or his hands is a respectable man. Though by bad laws he may be badly clothed and badly housed and badly fed, and those who do not work for their living but who fatten upon the labour of others are not respectable people, but on the contrary are thieves and rogues and vagabonds, though they may wear fine linen and fare sumptuously every day. Though they may wear crowns upon their heads and have swords hanging at their tails. Though they maybe called Lords and Dukes and Marquisses and Viscounts and Right Reverend Fathers in God and Knights of the Garter and Grooms of the Stole [in charge of the monarch's ceremonial dressing, personal attendance and associated staff. Ed.] and Lords of the Bedchamber and all the other mummery and flummery and humbuggery.

I therefore will address you Mr Chairman and friends as respectable people, for I presume that with the exception of a sprinkling there and a sprinkling there and a few there and a few there of despicable wretches who have hired themselves for blood money, with the exception of these creatures we are all respectable people. I hope I work for my living. If Lord John Russell wants to know what I am, I am a Merchant in the City of London and though perhaps I have not much Rhino [slang word for 'money'. Ed.] I am perhaps more respectable than many other Merchants, for I do go to market with ready money, sell fish about the streets, and if Lord John Russell wants to be a customer I will sell him a Pike cheap (loud cheers) or if the Treasury is almost exhausted which I dare say it nearly is. If the Exchequer is very low indeed I am a charitable man, though our friend Shaw the other night said he would not be so merciful as I am. If the Treasury is so very low and Lord John Russell cannot afford to buy a Pike I will give him one.

I was going to say that we live in queer times. I say again, it is a privilege to live in these times, but let us not forget that there is a danger also in living in these times. Some of the men that I invited today to speak on this platform perhaps think so. However, there is one thing we must not forget before all - and above all - namely that we live in times when every man expects each other to do his duty. These are the times for duty. We must perform our duty. If we perform out duty well, generations yet unborn will bless us. If we perform our duty ill, generations yet unborn will curse us. What is that duty? The *Northern Star* of last week says our duty is to sympathise with Ireland. The *Northern Star* says well. Is our duty to end there? My friends, our duty is to sympathise with Ireland, yes. Our duty is to pity Ireland, yes, and our duty is to help Ireland and I will tell you how we will help her the best way we can. I am not going to tell you Gentlemen or Friends in God's name get arms - for that is sedition. I am not going to say in God's name get Pikes, for that is felony. But I am going to say in God's name get umbrellas for the rains may fall. I am going to say in God's name get greatcoats for the winter is coming and you might catch cold. I am not going to tell you my opinion of the Government of this Country, you will pretty well know that - but I will give you the opinion of somebody else, and as this man is a long way off, I don't think that the Government will be able to catch him. And that is the Editor of the *New York Herald*. I am reading from a stamped newspaper - *The Times* - the most loyal paper in all the world, and therefore there is no treason in that. This is what Brother Jonathan [an American expression for the American people in general. Ed.] thinks of the British Government. They say we are a nation. You and I, we are a nation, say they are grovelling in abject slavery.

"There is a shame a narrow oligarchy is grinding the masses of our population to powder. It takes taxes and plunders the State for its own lucre and ambition. The Church, the Law, the Army the Navy and the Crown are kept up only to satiate its hungry maw and aggrandise its powers."

"The Middle Classes", says Brother Jonathan, - I don't say so – "are either the slaves or toadies - the lower class only slaves. Chartism is the only natural and true expression of the popular feeling; the unconcealed wish of the majority of the people is for a Republic, and they are only kept in check by the terrors of military force."

And now something to the point that has called us together tonight. We will quote Brother Jonathan again because they cannot catch him:

"If ever there were a people", says the Editor of the *New York Herald*, which mark you is the organ of the war party, and the war party in America is now getting the ascendancy, and that is another significant fact,

"If ever there were a people who had cause to rise and strike down their tyrants, the Irish are that people. If ever there was a time to do it, the present is it. The crisis may be delayed until after Harvest, but we are inclined to think that it will come then beyond all peradventure. They will gain an accession to their ranks from Mr Mitchell's conviction and transportation of thousands who have heretofore opposed their movements and if after rising in arms they can but hold their ground for five or six weeks their example will assuredly be followed by the Chartists."

I don't say so, it is the Editor of the *New York Herald*,

"and the result will be the downfall of the great tyrant of the Universe, one of the most corrupt, tyrannical grinding and despotic governments that Providence ever permitted to afflict a world. In this downfall the nobility and aristocracy the well fed puppets of the government, they who have lived on the fat of the land and revelled in luxury purchased by the sweat and anguish of a nation will be crushed to atoms."

If I am not detaining you too long, I will read you another extract because you know I was told the other night that I was a very good General that I should not get into quod [slang word for 'prison'. Ed.]. It will be more luck than judgement, in my opinion. However, the last evening I spoke I only prayed something. It does not say in the Act that we must not pray. It only says that we must not imagine, compass or devise. Tonight I am only reading something. The gagging Bill does not say we must not read. So you see I like to do everything according to Law. Brother Jonathan says again,

"By the last arrival from England we have some indications of the policy which England has shaped and which from all appearances she is determined to pursue. It is not a direct open and honest policy such as Russia has marked out, but a mean pitiful sneaking and underhand system of petty intrigue; Machiavellian deception which has always characterised her government from time immemorial. It is the same system which she has so successfully thus far used towards Ireland, and by which she has been enabled to retain her dominion over that island, in despite of the wishes of its people and in direct contravention of all principles of justice human and divine. Fearing the powerful Republic its increase, its stability and its future greatness, and knowing herself to be powerless to oppose any obstacle in its way, this wicked, atrocious and diabolical government has embarked in a policy which would disgrace the Thugs of India. She dare not meet the Republic in the field, and there manfully and honourably dispute the spread of the principles of free government in Europe. The first shock of battle would show her nakedness and prostrate her. But she can play the assassin; she can stab her enemy in the back as she has done on former occasions and as she is attempting to do again. But it will be seen with what success eventually. The policy she has determined upon is to send abroad her agents for the purpose of intriguing with the people and with the governments of the continental nations. Of putting the people against the governments and the governments against the people. Of inciting the masses to rise for their rights and inciting the governments when the masses have risen to massacre them as has been done in Naples. There is not only every probability but it is almost a moral certainty that the late dreadful massacres in the city of Naples were the work of this treacherous and mean government through the agency of its intrigues. At the present time there is no doubt that England has her agents scattered throughout all Europe."

Of course she has. She has them scattered in Milton Street Theatre.

"Whose missions are of this character and who if successful would deluge Europe with the blood of the people and re-establish amid carnage and desolation monarchy in France and stop the progress of the principles of free government from making further headway in Europe. These are the despicable and underhand means which this assassin government has resorted to overthrow France, not daring as we have before stated, to measure lances with the giant Republic."

Now the *Times* says in answer to this that England has no more to dread from the navies of France than she has from the armies of America, and that she will meddle with the internal affairs of neither. Not because she dreads the strength of either, but because, and I think so too, but because she respects the rights of nations and recognises the value of peace. Now there is an important question in the Bill. Is Ireland up? I am not in the Cabinet. I am not in the Council. Oh yes, I know Lord John Russell was found guilty once by a Galway jury but there has been more juries than the Galway jury set about Lord John Russell. But the question is asked in the bill, is Ireland up? I think you will all own that she has been down long enough, and another thing you will own too. I think it is time she was up, and if she don't get up herself do one man serve her right for being down; serve any willing slave right; serve any one right that kisses the chains that bind them. It is only a shame that the innocent should suffer with the guilty, and that those who pant for liberty should still be in bondage while some are slaves at heart. But I hope that Ireland is not a slave at heart and the time is fast approaching perhaps at this very moment she is at it - and if she is, God of the suffering poor defend the right.

In ancient times the question was asked, 'How long oh Lord, how long shall tyrants reign?' I ask that question again. I say, how long oh Lord shall tyrants reign? Tyrants have reigned in Ireland for seven centuries nearly, and I hope that those who have mocked her sufferings and starved her, may now meet with the reward they merit, whoever they are. But what would Ireland do if she had her nationality, say some people. What has that to do with me as an

Englishman? The Irish have a right to govern themselves. If they govern themselves ill the rod will fall upon their own backs. Why should eight millions of Irishmen merely because they are Irishmen, be called the most stupid people upon the face of the earth? If they govern themselves ill they will have all the consequences. If they govern themselves well they will have the advantage of all being well. But let the Irish nation as every other nation, govern itself by its own laws.

Some people say what have the English to do with it. The English I consider if they are Democrats at heart, have to do with everything that is oppressive and unjust; they have raised their voice against injustice and oppression in Poland. Why not raise their voice when injustice and oppression is perpetrated in Ireland?

Lord John Russell said yesterday when some of the Irish members of the House of Commons were told by his Lordship to go to Ireland where they were wanted to make peace, they said,

"But will you not give us some remedial measures, something by way of an olive branch to take to Ireland?"

"No," said Lord John Russell, "You must go without any remedial measures at all."

I say the government are acting either very roguish or very insane, and therefore I say openly and advisedly that neither a roguish government nor an insane government ought to exist. But the same Gentleman says we do not want any reform.

Why Gentlemen, I am ready here to assert and as I love discussion I would discuss it with anybody that there is something rotten in the political state of England that from the crown of the head to the sole of the foot there is nothing but wounds and putrefying sores. That Monarchy, Aristocrats, Lords, Freetraders, Special Constables and Blue Devils [name for the police due to their blue uniform. Ed.] have all done that which they ought not to have done, and have left undone that which they ought to do; and if there is one monopoly more than another in this country, it is the monopoly of legislation. One in seven has no voice in this country, and while that is so we are virtually slaves. If there is one abomination in Ireland more than another it is the English Church as by law established, and I advise you as soon as you have three pence about you to read the Black Book of England published by Cleave [*The Black Book of England:*

exhibiting the existing state, policy, and administration of the United Kingdom. With lists of the chief recipients of public pay in church and state. London, 1847. Ed.] and learn and mark well and inwardly digest too, and you will find that Lord John Russell was very foolish, and [was] told this too when he stated that the people of England wanted no reform. But some of them tell you that the great cause is the surplus population in England and Ireland.

That is just what I believe myself, and I think that it is about first time that the government and I ever agreed. But so it is. There is too many Bishops. There is too much aristocracy. There is too many drones to live upon the bees. I wish to God they would emigrate. I would not send them to heaven, though there is no question about that, for they would not be let in. Nor I would not send them to hell, for I should not be uncharitable enough to do that. But I would send them to some remote quarter of the globe and let no one go there except the Bishops and those persons. I say that a system of emigration is a very good thing, and the sooner these fellows emigrate the better. With these few remarks I beg leave to reiterate the sentiment whether it be treason or felony or sedition or no, I beg leave to reiterate the sentiment that is now in my bosom, for I always like to say what I mean, and mean what I say, notwithstanding the consequences that may ensue, for the truth ought to be spoken.

I reiterate the sentiment that Ireland is justified in rising up in arms against those who have oppressed her, and God grant that she may win; and I say in the language of the poet of last week:

> *'Down with the Aristocratic Slavery*
> *Up with the Republican Bravery.' "*

Bezer then addressed the jury (having no council) in response to the Attorney-General. He admitted that he was a Chartist, and said the country was labouring; and if the Whig government, which had so often for its own purposes encouraged agitation, thought to put down the expression of the feeling of the working population of the country by such prosecutions as these they were very much mistaken, for they might rely on it that the people would become more determined to obtain their rights by that sort of treatment. It had been made a ground of complaint against him that he had read an extract from an American paper to an audience of 1,000 persons; but they should not forget that he was reading from a newspaper that had perhaps 30,000 subscribers, and if he was to blame for reading it, he thought *The Times* ought also to be prosecuted for printing it in the first instance, as, if they had not printed it, he could not have read it....

In conclusion he described the prosecutions that had been instituted by the Government as merely intended to destroy the right of freedom of speech in this country, and he called upon the jury, as members of the middle class of society, not to lend themselves to such a proceeding by convicting him upon the present charge.

In reply, the Attorney-General said that the defence which had been made by the defendant confirmed the opinion he had originally expressed of the dangerous description of ability which he possessed.... The manner in which he had artfully read the exciting extract from the American paper, and omitted the comments upon it, giving the bane but omitting the antidote, likewise showed his dangerous ability for mischief, particularly as he expected thereby to escape from punishment. The Attorney-General praised the *Times* and most other papers for the generous and noble manner in the preservation of the public peace. After summing up, the jury returned a verdict of Guilty. Bezer was sentenced to be imprisoned in the House of Correction [Newgate Prison] for two years, and to pay a fine of £10.

Note: John Shaw's trial was held on the 18 September 1848, and the account of the speech that he gave adds to, and complements Bezer's . See www.oldbaileyonline.org

A corridor in Newgate Prison. (*Illustrated London News*, 1850

3.

RELEASE FROM NEWGATE
AND AFTERMATH

Newgate Prison on the left, looking towards Old Bailey

Bezer was released in April 1850 upon recognisance in the sum of £100, with two sureties of £50 each and to keep the peace and be of good behaviour for five years.

During 1849 Bezer and Shaw had requested an increase in light and fire, the use of pen, paper and ink, and an alteration in diet. It was then considered that they were 'misconducting themselves' by writing to and receiving letters from Chartists imbued with their dangerous politics, and other refractory conduct. Their privileges were suspended. Responding to a petition on their behalf, the authorities stated that they were confined in a block of fifteen old cells – not 'condemned' cells as was thought, and that Newgate had no 'condemned cells' of that description. The petition was referred to the Gaol Committee. Although Bezer probably found the conditions barely tolerable, John Shaw, an undertaker by trade in Gloucester Street, Commercial Road, had been used to better things.

In a letter dated December 11, 1848, from his No. 8 Cell at Newgate to George Julian Harney, he had complained bitterly about his gout, the cold, and his damp linen (there being no fire). (*Harney Papers*)

Punishment cell, Newgate Prison (*Illustrated London News 1850*)

On April 22, 1850, a large meeting was convened at the South London Chartist Hall, Webber Street, Southwark, under the auspices of the National Charter Association. During this meeting the recently released Chartists were welcomed to the platform amidst cheering. Bezer addressed the meeting, saying that he was a most grateful man, the Whigs had been very very kind to him, and he exhibited his gratitude by attending the very first Chartist meeting after his liberation. (Laughter.) His eighty-six weeks' confinement had not reformed him, except it had changed his mind a little; when he went to prison he thought his principles were right, but now he was sure they were. (Cheers.)

A brother radical had met him coming to the meeting, and shook him cordially by the hand, and asked him did he mean to cause the meeting to laugh? He hoped the meeting would remember that, although eighty-six weeks' incarceration had not broken his heart, yet he could not conceive that Newgate's sombre walls were calculated to enliven his spirits or make him gay - (Hear-hear.) - more especially when he remembered he had left their honest uncompromising friend (John Shaw) immured within its walls. He had heard too, (what should he, as a loyal man call them,) wicked speeches. He was not a learned man, although he had been called to the bar - (laughter) - and when there, his learned brother, her Majesty's Attorney-General, had said, pointing to him (Mr. Bezer):

"The prisoner has positively offered to sell Lord John Russell a pike - a pike, yes gentlemen, a pike." (Roars of laughter.)

Ah, it was easy for them to laugh, but allow him to say it put all the old ladies in court into a state of "*Terroris extremis.*" (Increased laughter.) Well, he had told them that he was not a learned man, but he had searched Johnson, Entick, and others, and had there found that a pike was a fish, and of course, by a parity of reasoning, a fish was a pike. (Laughter.) Well, as they all knew he was a City merchant, he dealt in fish, and, of course, merchant-like, wished to have the patronage of the first Minister of the Crown; but instead of giving him (Mr. Bezer) an order for the pike, he had given him an order for the "Stone Jug." (Laughter and applause.) ["Stone Jug" slang for a prison cell. Ed.] When there he had been visited by the magistrates; one in particular said:

"Oh, you are Bezer - you are a fool - I don't pity you - you not only get yourself into trouble, but you endeavour to get others into trouble by your talk. Ah, 'twas lucky for you that you did not attempt to march from Kennington Common, for I suppose you were there, or you would all have been annihilated, for I had command of the bridges; one did come roaring out, I am a Chartist - brandishing his stick - I took it from him and threw it into the water; can I do anything for you?"

Yes, he wished to see his wife –

"For what reason?"

Because he was a husband and father. (Loud cheers.)

"Oh! that's no reason."

Four times had this "Commander of Bridges" visited him and repeated the same tale; but he hoped the meeting would not think the "Commander" was Mr. Alderman Farebrother. (Loud laughter.)...

Mr. Bezer then called for three cheers for John Shaw, which were heartily given, and resumed his seat greatly applauded.

On the following day, April 23, a meeting was held at the John Street Institution on behalf of the Chartists who were still imprisoned. A number of notable Chartists addressed the meeting, including Bronterre O'Brien, G.W.M. Reynolds, George Julian Harney, Walter Cooper, Gerald Massey and Bezer.

Bezer was greeted with a most rapturous welcome, and said that on the 28 July 1848, he was on the platform of the Milton Street Institution, but on the same date in 1849 he had found himself in quite a different place. And why? because he had spoken freely, and he meant what he then said. (Hear.) He recollected one sentence he had uttered to the government reporters; it was –

"They were there, not because they feared the government, but because the government feared the uneducated costermonger," (great cheering.)

and his saying had been verified. When brother Shaw got out he should have a tale to tell them. (Three cheers were called for, and heartily given, for John Shaw.) On the occasion some of his friends had advised him to go out of the way, and he had taken himself to Highgate; only five persons knew where he was, and one of them had proved a Judas, by selling the secret for sixty pieces of copper - yes, for five shillings. (Hear, hear.) Well, he was arrested, tried, as it was called, and convicted, of course; and what was he charged with? Why, conspiring against Her Majesty, her crown, and dignity. (Laughter.) Now, really, he had never mentioned the little lady's name; but he had told the people, they - the producers of wealth - were responsible. Of course this was seditious - truth and sedition being synonymous terms. (Loud cheers.) Well, he was now out of prison, in mind and principle a wiser man than when he went in, - (cheers) - and to use a lady's expression - "He was as well as could be expected," - (laughter) - and so he ought to be, considering that in eighty-six weeks he had swallowed, upon a fair computation, three hogsheads of skilly. (Laughter.) [Some 165 gallons of gruel. Ed.] Well, it appeared that Popes ran away, Kings had their whiskers shaved off, - (laughter) - and stand ye firm, for the poet has written:

"Mitres and Thrones from this world shall be hurled
And Peace and Brotherhood through the universe prevail."

A Dining Ward, Newgate Prison. (*Illustrated London News* 1850)

THE PRISONER'S PRAYER.

Bezer was inwardly very religious, was baptised at the age of 16, and attended a non-conformist chapel regularly where, according to his autobiography he progressed to instructing. Later he became a Dissenter - one who refuses to conform to the doctrines of the established church.

From the *Christian Socialist*, 1850.
(Written in one of the Condemned Cells of Newgate.)

"Let the sighing of the prisoner come before Thee."

Psalm 79-2

God, everlasting great Creator, One
　　　Whose ways mysterious are, past finding out,
Yet earth and air, and sea, and the bright sun,
　　　And all creation's works, prove beyond doubt,
　　　　Unvarying beneficence and love, -
Permit, O Lord, a weak and bruised reed
　　　To praise Thy glorious name for mercies past,
And pray for aid in all his future need;
　　　Help him, on Thee his every care to cast,
　　　　And look to Thee alone - Father above!

Lord I have sinn'd - sinn'd deeply - from my youth
　　　Spirit and flesh have battled long and sore,
And flesh have often conquered - of a truth
　　　I can do nothing in this ceaseless war -
　　　　In me (that is, my flesh) dwells no good thing,
But in Thine own revealed I will read,
　　　That Thou wilt e'en forgive the vile, the base:
In mercy Thou delightest, and I plead
　　　Thy promises of pardon and of grace,
　　　　To Thee a broken contrite heart I bring.

Thy chastening hand is on me: - Shepherd spare
　　　Thy poor wandering sheep!　Thy stripes are light
Compared to those I merit, yet forbear
　　　Compassionate Creator!　Let the night
　　　　Be short, and morning soon again appear!
Open the prison doors and set me free!
　　　Yet thou must pardon if I ask amiss,
For I am weak and tempted; let me be
　　　Resigned, and humbly learn the rod to kiss,
　　　　Whate'er thy will, oh give me strength to bear!

And when our toils and cares on earth are o'er,
　　　O may we meet in the broad realms above,
And with our friends and dear ones gone before,
　　　Join in the thrilling chorus "God is love"
Around the great white throne, and part no more.
　　　No prison bars or bolts, no night is there,
No anguish and no sin - all, all is joy -
　　　Prepare us for that blissful change, prepare-
All earthly, vain, and sensual thoughts destroy,
　　　And make us meet to drink that fountain pure.

Bless all Thy ministering servants, bless,
    Whate'er their creed, (to me 'tis all the same
So that they work for Thee in faithfulness,
    And not for Mammon, or for earthly fame);
With grace and wisdom every one endow'd;
        Hasten the time when every one shall know Thy
            name,
Virtue and truth shall conquer lies and vice,
    Men follow Christ: - so peace on earth proclaim,
And make this glorious globe a paradise; -
    'Tis only sin that mars its beauties now.
Show pity to the poor mistaken ones,
    Victims of evil training; - pardon all
Within these walls, and let earth's favoured sons
    Take careful heed, (or they too, may soon fall;)
Their weaker brethren educate and save.
    Tyrants of every clime and age, beware!
The last tremendous sessions draweth near,
    The great eternal magistrate is there;
Judges and criminals on earth appear,
    The rich, the poor, the freeman, the slave!

Banish all malice from Thy servant's heart
    Teach me to pray for those who do me ill,
Let each revengeful angry thought depart,
    And even while they harm me love me still,
And though they smite, learn not to smite again.
    My leader be Thy well-beloved Son -
The image of Thyself, the good, the great,
    The sinner's friend, the meek, the lowly one,
Oh! may I ever love to imitate!
    Give me the mind of Jesus Christ.   Amen.
                    J. J. BEZER.

Newgate Prison Chapel. (*Illustrated London News 1850*)

The Chapel Yard, Newgate Prison. (*Illustrated London News 1850*)

References

'Autobiography of one of the Chartist Rebels of 1848.' Serialised in *The Christian Socialist*, 1851, but not completed due to *The Christian Socialist* being discontinued. Reprinted in *Testaments of Radicalism*, edited by David Vincent. London, Europa, 1977.

Harney Papers, ed. Black & Black, Van Gorcam, Assen, 1969.

Illustrated London News, February 23, 1850, p.131, State of Newgate.

Northern Star and National Trades' Journal. December 12, 1849, p.5. Bezer and Shaw in Newgate. Conditions.

Northern Star and National Trades' Journal. April 27, 1850, p.1. Meeting at the South London Chartist Hall following the release of the Chartists from prison. (See also David Shaw's biography of Gerald Massey, chapter 2.)

Regina v. Bezer. Indictment. Central Criminal Court, August Sessions 1848. (Treasury Solicitor and HM Procurator General. Papers TS 11/1119).

Times, July 27, 1848, p.8. John Shaw and Bezer at meeting.

Times, August 24, 1848, p.7. Account of prosecution of John Shaw.

Times, August 29, 1848, p.7. Brief account of Bezer's trial together with the other defendants, Snell, Crowe, and Bryson.

Times, April 20, 1850, p.7. Item on Bezer's release from prison.

Leather Lane, c. 1870

AFTERMATH

The occasion of Bezer's release from Newgate in April 1850 together with a number of other Chartists, was used to promote the Chartist cause. A meeting was convened by the provisional committee of the National Charter Association on the 23 April 1850, at the John Street Institute. Thirteen of the released Chartists mounted the platform, and committee members, including Bronterre O'Brien and George Julian Harney made spirited addresses. Bezer was introduced, and addressed the packed hall amid loud cheering. (*Northern Star*, 27April 1850.)

The Literary and Scientific Institute, 23 John Street, Fitzroy Square
(*Illustrated London News*, 15 April, 1848.)

The picture shows the Chartist convention preparing for the Kennington Common demonstration held on the 10 April 1848. The building, according to W.E. Adams, was thought originally to have been a chapel.

Following the collapse of the Kennington meeting, the authorities took a much more lenient view of subversive lectures, as the threat of organised violence had considerably diminished, and Bezer lost no time in continuing his Chartist activities. The *Northern Star* (4 May, 1850) noted that Bezer was commencing a series of weekly lectures at the 'Old Dolphin,' Old Street, St. Luke. His first lecture to be 'What can I do for Liberty?'

Later, at a public meeting of the National Charter Association Executive to discuss the Foreign Policy of Government Ministers, Bezer came forward amid much cheering. He said that as regards ministers and their foreign policy, he thought they cared more for people that were far away than they did for those at home. He held in his hand *The Young American*, a Republican paper, which paper was the advocate of social rights. He then read several extracts showing that poverty and pauperism prevailed in the States and that even the Republican institutions were not complete if confined to mere politics. That showed the necessity for social rights, such as the nationalisation of the land etc. Bezer continued by quoting many great authors in favour of equality of rights, and appealed to the audience not to heed mere names, but to stand by principles. He sat down to loud applause. (*Northern Star*, 6 July 1850.)

In July 1850 the Metropolitan District Council resolved that localities take a benefit with a view of placing the victim [as a political martyr] John James Bezer in a small way of business. Bezer said he should like the joint trades of greengrocer and fishmonger. The Council considered that if the sum exceeded £10, the excess could be devoted to other political martyrs. Bezer thought, with that, and an already promised amount, he could make a fair start with £10.

The following month the question of improved circulation of information was brought up at a National Charter Association meeting. Bezer was called to the Chair, and discussions were raised re the dissemination of democratic knowledge via tracts, periodicals and newspapers. It was noted that many shopkeepers refused to expose *The Red Republican* for sale, or obtain it when ordered. Bezer pointed to the necessity of extending political and social knowledge to prevent the people in future being fleeced by parliament voting an immense Palace to an infant in his ninth year, and give five thousand pounds for stables for the Prince of Wales' horses, nine or ten years hence. This was supported by Bronterre O'Brien. Mr Gerald Massey amidst loud cheers, came forward and suggested a number of broad general axioms, such as "All men are brethren," etc. and said that he thought some broad basis of this description might be laid, on which all could stand in the common band of unity. He said that in six months not less than eight associations had been established, and invoked them to press onward in the good cause of democracy, burying feuds in the dust. (Cheers.) (*Northern Star*, 10 August, 1850)

During that month, Bezer had been making arrangements for a lecture tour throughout the Midlands. His general subjects for the lectures were advertised in the *Red Republican* and *Northern Star* as:

- The sufferings of himself and fellow-victims in prison.

- The principles of social and democratic reform.

- The united organisation of social and democratic reformers to obtain the Charter.

His home address was given as 32 Bartholomew Close, Smithfield. [Still on maps today, off 'Little Britain', but redeveloped.]

Commencing at the New Hall, Northampton on Monday 19 August, his subject was Political and Social Reform, with Revelations of his Imprisonment. *The Northern Star* (24 August, 1850) reported that Bezer's "happy vein of treating the subject gained him continued plaudits."

Then to Leicester for two lectures the following day, at which 1,000 persons were stated to be present. He continued on to Loughborough, Sherwood Forrest, Sutton-in-Ashfield and Arnold. At Holbrook Moor, two pieces written by him whilst in Newgate prison were sung, and he spoke on the People's Charter and his treatment in Newgate.

Following Bezer's lecture tour, complaints were being made regarding the treatment of other Chartist prisoners. On the 8 October 1850 a public meeting was held in the Broadway, Westminster, for the purpose of hearing statements from several Chartists who had been held in Newgate, Tothill Fields and Horsemonger Lane prisons.

John Arnott, as Secretary to the Victim Committee of the National Charter Association had been in communication with Thomas Wakley M.P. for Finsbury, regarding the treatment of the prisoners. Mr Wakley had referred the matter to Sir George Grey who had been informed by the Secretary of the Home Office that, following enquiries, he had been assured that the prison regulations had been conformed with. This was despite the fact that two Chartists had died in prison, victims of ill treatment.

The mother of one of the victims gave an account to the Coroner. She stated that she went to visit her son, and found him in a prostrate state. Enquiring what nourishment he had received, the officer on duty said that he had plenty of soda water. Upon asking if her son could be allowed a little arrow-root, the officer replied that he would not take it. But on asking her son, he said yes, he would take it. Two hours later some three tablespoonfuls were brought to her, which her son took. On visiting the next day, he told her that he had received nothing since her last visit. He died the following day.

Ward for condemned prisoners, Newgate. (*Illustrated London News 1850*)

Bezer who was present as one of the victims, said that imprisonment had only sent him there as a Chartist, and it has sent him out a Republican. He said that the first speaker (Mr Shaw) had suffered extremely, and had for some time been compelled to go upon crutches. There was a classification of prisoners in Newgate, of which the public had little knowledge, but the classification was not one as regarded the nature of their crimes, but as regarded the weight of their pockets. There were in Newgate prison fifteen condemned cells, and he and Shaw were confined in two of these for twelve months, until rheumatism and illness laid them both on their backs. He certainly tried to make himself rather a troublesome customer, and among other things, on the anniversary of Charles the Second, he refused to go to chapel, as he said he didn't want to return thanks for any such matter, as he thought Charles the Second ought to have been treated just the same as his father had been [executed! Ed.]. They were always told they must conform to the rules of the prison, but these rules, although he had often asked for them, they never yet could see.

It was reported that Bezer continued with his experiences at considerable length. (*Northern Star*, 12 October, 1850.)

On the 26 October Bezer commenced as a newsagent. This was probably a rethink of his previous suggestion of a job as greengrocer and fishmonger that he had given at the Metropolitan District Council meeting. In November he gave his address for this as 6 Sycamore Street, Old Street, St Luke's.

About this time George Julian Harney had received a cleverly rhymed letter with a verse and cartoon from 'M.P.' who stated he had received it with a request that it be forwarded to Harney. It was signed Brougham and Vaux, but was thought unlikely to have been written by him. Henry Brougham (1778 – 1868) was 1st Baron Brougham and Vaux, and a radical reformer.

The cartoon was a parody of the "Arms of the British Monarchy", with the verse being an 'explanation' of the items on the Arms (*Red Republican*, 26 October 1850). These items are shown below:

LORD BROUGHAM

TO THE EDITOR OF THE RED REPUBLICAN

You, like all clever men, dear Harney!
Know I abominate all blarney,
Tow'rds high and low, to friends and foes.
In place or out, in verse or prose,
In foreign climates or at home,
I'm always just the same plain Brougham.
I hate all flattery; not that I
Would hit a friend upon the sly.
I speak my mind out like a man,
And make a hit just when I can....(1)
Though sometimes pausing on the brink,
I don't perhaps say all I think:
For I'm not spiteful nor sarcastic.
But having a nature very plastic   (2)
I turn my talents multifarious,
To objects useful, vast, and various.
Well, Harney!   I admire your Red
Republican; and so I said
To my friend Lyndhurst, who agreed
With me, 'twas very red indeed.

And thereupon I write you this
Concise and terse and brief epis-
Tle, (you'll excuse this funny nick
In the word's middle! 'Tis a trick
We poets have: myself and Wakley,
Who hold our jawing-tackle slackly);
Partly became, I blush to own,
Though there are few things I've not done,-
And well; say better; I have yet
One sad omission to regret:
That never for the People's sake
I've worked till now.   So prithee take
This letter as a part amends.
Henceforth we shall, I trust, be friends;
And as I still am hale and hearty,
Untrammel'd too by place or party,
I'll give your side a turn or two,
Old boy! Won't that astonish you?
But to the purpose of this letter.
(Few men, I think could write a better:
The engraving is my own design,
Maclise allows it's very fine,-
And by myself cut in the wood,
My first attempt, and rather good).
On my old quest of useful knowledge,
I search'd of late the Herald's college:
Wishing to learn if I could trace
Brougham and Vaux's shining race ...(3)
To history's unexampled Guy.
I found him out.(4)   How history
Has slandered him!   It slanders me!
Well, what d'ye think I chanced to see
Among a lot of queer old rubbish,
Hid in a corner rather grubbish?
(I love such corners!) How I laugh'd:
'Twas our KINGS' ARMS' original draft.
And all in herald jargon writ:
You'd never have decipher'd it.
I did, and found it pleasant too;
And now translate the same for you.
I might have given it in plain prose,...(5)
But write verse easier; - So here goes.

The Arms of Britain's monarchy, by loyal Britons prized,
'Tis surely time their bearings were made plain and vulgarized:
That even the meanest British slave, or the nearest to the Brutes,
May know exactly what they mean, those royal attributes.
The herald's coat's a bishop's frock, to show the "right divine,"
Which is somehow got at through the Church, and quite direct the
    line;
And the bishop's stirring in the coat, with a swaggering, tipsy gait,
- For his foot is on the poor, - 'tis not that he's intoxicate.
The poor man lies right in his way, with his face hid in the earth,
As if, spite of his crown of thorns, he isn't of much worth; -
But turn to the bishop's blazonry, and feast your vacant look
On the royal quarterings: here they are, as in the herald book.

For England's lions - donkeys, sanguine, on a field of gold;
For Ireland's harp - a peasant strung upon a gallows old;
The Scottish quarter is not seen, but there can be little doubt,
It's a rampant donkey, sanguine (all the donkeys look starved out).

For supporters - on the sinister side's a lion of the law. (6)
With spectacles and learned wig and awful breadth of jaw;
And dexter side the unicorn, with a death's head in his hat,
And saddled back, - he seems to bid the bishop mount on that.

The whole's surmounted for a crest, with the bonnet and the phiz
Of our most gracious sovereign: and very plain it is -
That the wreath of German sausages hangs there in honour of him
To whom a grateful nation owes so many a royal limb. (7)
The motto still is as of old. - "God and my right:" but "God"
Lies under the couchant lawyer's paws; and the armed brute has
     trod
On "Right." There's little alteration you can see in all these
     things
Since heralds first found monsters out and liken'd them to kings.

> You'll publish this: t'will make some laugh,
> Some think. And for my autograph, -
> I'm not so vain as Wellingon
> Who gives his mark to every one;
> But you can sell it - the proceeds
> May help your advertizing needs.
> Yours, without prejudice or flaw,
> Fraternally ever,
> Brougham and Vaux.

(1   Pretty often, I guess.
2   "Plastick - that facility which can form or fashion anything," –Bailey's Dictionary.
3   Does he mean by the aristocratic slime, slug-like?
4   Guy Fawkes, or Vaux. His lordship's not so green as we thought.
5   Unconscious that he was writing verse before. The sublime unconsciousness of genius, according to Mr. Carlyle.
6   There seems some mistake here. Or, has the noble writer shrewdly altered the relative position of the supporters? It is true the law has grown more dexterous and the sword rather left-handed of late. Perhaps not knowing the process of printing, he has forgotten to reverse the drawing.
7   As we say, a limb of the law. I was called a limb when I was a child.)

The cartoon, together with the letter and verse obviously appealed to Bezer's sense of humour. He had it reprinted, and advertised it for sale at his home address, Sycamore Street, in the following fortnight's *Red Republican* for one halfpenny, or 7d per quire for Trade.

Bezer was also quick to take advantage of the Christian Socialists, having been introduced to them by Walter Cooper. In two advertisements in December 1850 issues of the *Christian Socialist*, he referred to himself by:

RECOMMENDATION EXTRAORDINARY!

J.J. BEZER, from Newgate!!
News Agent and dealer in Periodicals.
No. 6, Sycamore Street, Old Street, St. Lukes.
Orders punctually attended to.

Continuing with his activities, later in the year he stood on the Polish Refugees Sub-committee of the Metropolitan Trades Committee. Then in January the following year, 1851, at a public meeting at the Literary Institute, Portman Square, he moved:

That the Executive of the National Charter Association as a body deserves the support of all true democrats. To make the agitation [for the Charter], they must join the Association, and prove by their zeal that they really were in earnest in their profession of a desire to raise themselves on the side of social society.

Persistent dissention between the locally powerful Manchester Chartists and the National Charter Association gave the NCA cause for continuing concern. A meeting was convened at the John Street Institute in February to receive a report of the Executive Committee relative to charges made at the Manchester Conference by Feargus O'Connor. Gerald Massey and others spoke, and Bezer moved:

That this meeting is further of opinion that the people's cause requires that their acknowledged leaders should be protected from insidious and indirect attacks and denunciations; and that it holds as despicable the conduct of any man and every man, whose practice it is to vaguely and treacherously arraign and denounce those leaders, and yet shrink from the responsibility of proof.

This received support, was applauded, and adopted.

The census record for 1851 shows the family at 6 Sycamore Street:
John Bezer, 34, News Agent. Jane S. Bezer, 34. Francis S. Bezer, 13. Emily D. Bezer, 7. Mary N. Bezer, 5, and Walter C. Bezer, 3.

Sycamore Street - noted on the map - was situated between Old Street and Goswell Road, and led from Rotten Row to Old Street. A small part of the street is still on maps today, with Rotten Row being renamed Crescent Row.

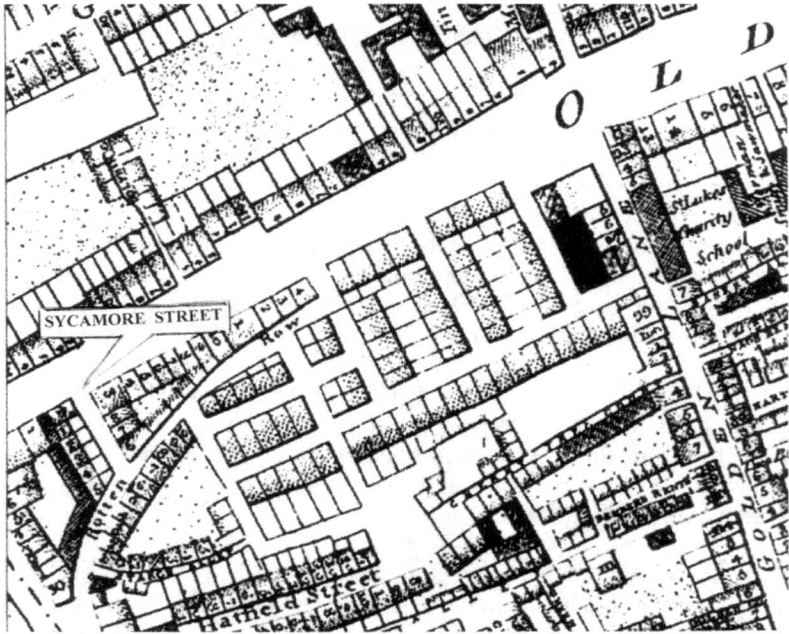

Sycamore Street, between Old Street and Rotten Row.
No 6 is at the corner.

The year of 1851 was made particularly notable by the Crystal Palace Exhibition in Hyde Park. However, Bezer prejudged this in a most negative manner. A lecture that he presented in March titled 'The Exhibition, what will be exhibited, and what is hidden', at the Rose and Crown, Colville Place, Tottenham Court Road, was reported by the *Northern Star*:

'Bezer ably dilated upon the false and hollow grandeur which would be exhibited to the visitors from abroad, whilst every endeavour would be made to banish poverty from their view.

They would see the Glass Palace glazed by unpaid and imprisoned glaziers. The enormous block of coal would be exhibited, but the poor miners would be hidden. Splendid silks would be there, but the weavers would be kept out of view. The productions of industry would be shown, but none of its due rewards. They would see an immense blue exhibition of 6,000 police, and 300 intensely blue, for the purpose of keeping peace, law and order, near the building. They would also see an immense red exhibition, headed by her Majesty's most confidential adviser - the Duke of Wellington. There would likewise be a great exhibition of rant, cant, and humbug. If they looked at the *Times* or *Chronicle*, they would see subscriptions called for to convert the poor Heathens who would be present at this Vanity Fair. If a poor Chartist attempted to speak of his wrongs, the blue and red exhibition would soon put him down, though they would be unable to put down the truths he was anxious to enforce.

The Exhibition would be a monument of hollow, empty extravagance, supported by physical force on one hand, and superstition on the other. The attempt to hide poverty by keeping the costermongers and others out of the streets was vain and futile. They would fail in their object, and only increase the number of Chartists'.

Mr Bezer, during a clever and humorous address, was much applauded. (*Northern Star*, 22 March 1851.)

Bezer's advance negative opinion of a grand exhibition can be compared with that of Gerald Massey's over-artistically positive and long account of the Manchester Art Treasures Exhibition of 1857. (Massey biography, chapter 3.)

Note: The Crystal Palace Exhibition sited in Hyde Park was open from 1 May - 15 October 1851. In size, it extended to an area six times that of St Paul's Cathedral. Following the exhibition, the building was disassembled and reopened in Sydenham in 1854.

Bezer's fourth son now arrived. John James Bezer was born on 16 May 1851 at 3 Sycamore Street. Bezer was listed as a 'Newsagent', and appears to have moved from No. 6 in that street.

At a public meeting later in July, at Finsbury, Bezer noted how even the most liberal of Press, excepting the *Northern Star* and other democratic journals, misrepresented and distorted every meeting of working men, when they condescended to notice them. When a jeweller's shop was broken into at Camberwell, during the meetings in 1848, though it was well known by the evidence on the trial that it was done by a gipsy, who knew nothing about Chartism - yet even *Lloyd's*, a professing liberal paper, headed their account of the trial with the words - 'Trial and Conviction of another Chartist Leader.'

Yet another meeting was convened shortly after that, for victims of the spy system of Whig government. This was held at the Dog and Duck Tavern, at the corner of Frith Street and Queen Street, Soho. Discussion was raised to adopt steps relative to the parliamentary enquiry into their treatment during the ensuing session. Many victims and relatives were present. Bezer moved:

That we, the political victims of 1848, do now form ourselves into an Association, for the purpose of exposing the period of our incarceration, and to prosecute, by means of Lord Dudley Stuart and other parliamentary friends and enquiry before the next session of parliament relative thereto, and thus prevent a repetition of much unconstitutional and impolitic treatment.

The Political Victims Association met a week later, at the Paragon Chapel. Bronterre O'Brien took the Chair. During discussions, Bezer stated that he was not allowed to see his wife for five months, although a prisoner in the next cell saw his sweetheart every other day - but then the respectability of his crime was no doubt the cause of the difference between them, the fellow having only violated two children under eight years of age.

By way of advertisement and support, in October, the Victims Committee presented 'A Democrat Concert' at the Two Chairmen, Wardour Street, Soho. Bezer was in the Chair. The *Northern Star* reported that a number of male and female democrats attended to give mirth to the proceedings. Mr Bezer with his usual drollery turning 'The Victims of '48' into 'The King, God bless him.' John Arnott and John Bedford Leno gave appropriate recitations.

From 9 August 1851 having been recommended by F.D. Maurice, Bezer took over as publisher of the *Christian Socialist* using the office of the Society for Promoting Working Men's Associations, at 183 Fleet Street. In 1830, William Cobbett had published his Rural Rides from that address, and in 1847, William Edwards, importer of Parisian novelties, occupied the premises. However, the journal ran into financial difficulties, and was discontinued in December of that year, although reviving temporarily from 3 January to 28 June the following year as the *Journal of Association.* That premature curtailment of Bezer's autobiography, as previously mentioned, leaves a gap in his story of some eight years, and he probably intended to continue the autobiography up to the time of his arrest.

At his Fleet Street office/bookshop, he also published the *Star of Freedom* (change of name from the *Star and National Trades' Journal* which, previous to that, was the famed *Northern Star and National Trades' Journal*), from Vol. I, no. 1, 8 May 1852, to Vol. I (new series), no. 4, 4 September 1852. George Julian Harney took over as publisher from issue no 5. The *Star of Freedom* ceased publication from 27 November, and Waller & Son, Booksellers then occupied the bookshop at 183 Fleet Street.

In 1851, the City Builders were forming an Association, and a Public Meeting was held at the Hall of Science, City Road on 1 December. Gerald Massey and Frederick Furnivall attended on behalf of the Society for Promoting Working Men's Associations. Walter Cooper was to have been the principal speaker on their behalf, but he had been injured in a railway accident. Bezer was also in attendance, and seconded a resolution concerning a general fall in wages with consequent degredation of working men in all trades. The resolution stated, 'This meeting believes the unrestricted and increasing competition in all branches of productive industry, to be the cause of their fall in wages.' It was reported (*Christian Socialist*, 13 December 1851) that Bezer - Publisher to the Society - after giving a humorous defence of the class of distributors to which he had belonged all his life, followed through an argument proposed by Mr. Furnivall in his resolutions. Bezer emphasised the necessity and duty of association on the highest grounds, and maintained that the only reason which made working men dislike religion was, that the professors of Christianity so seldom acted up to their principles. He ended by asking what working men would be able to do with association when they had also got the vote, seeing the wonders they had already done without it?

Bezer also continued with his Chartist activities, and was one of nine elected to serve on the Executive of the National Charter Association for 1852. In January 1852 he lectured at the Literary Institution, Leicester Place, Little Saffron Hill, on 'Association among the poor; the only remedy for conspiracy among the rich.'

On 13 February 1852, Bezer's son, John James Bezer, aged 9 months, died of 'Teething Convulsions' at 10 Milford Lane, Strand, St Cement Danes, where the family were then living. Bezer is listed as a 'Bookseller'.

Following an adjourned Conference on 3 March 1852, the National Reform Association held an evening Aggregate public meeting at St. Martin's Hall, Long Acre. A number of prominent M.P.'s were present. During the proceedings, the Chairman, Mr. J. Hume M.P. made several comments that received support from the audience. One such expressed the tone of the meeting:

> ..the House of Commons did not represent the people; that the rule was placed in the hands of the aristocracy. If all classes did not participate in the election of those who formed the House of Commons, it could not be expected that the House of Commons should act fairly towards all classes...

Sir Charles Napier who was present, also called for radical reform, and hoped that when the present Ministry was turned out of office, as he most sincerely hoped, he trusted to see a good Administration composed of real Radical Reformers, who would present a bill worthy of the acceptance of the people of England.

A resolution was proposed and seconded,

> That this meeting believes radical Parliamentary reform to be the great practical want of the day, and, while declaring the maintenance of free trade, records its conviction that freedom of trade would have been impregnable if the suffrage had been placed upon a truly national basis, and that, in common with other equally important questions, free trade can only be finally decided when the House of Commons is made a real representation of the people.

Bezer, as a working man, rose and proposed as an amendment, the addition of the words:

> That the only principle of Parliamentary reform recognised by this meeting as just is the enactment of manhood suffrage, guaranteed by the ballot, short parliaments, equal electoral districts, no property qualification, and payment of representatives. (Great cheering.)

He agreed with the greater part of what had been said that evening. He agreed also that those who were amenable to the laws ought to have a voice in making those laws (cheers); that taxation and representation ought to go together, that it was especially important to the poor man to be represented, which meant, if it meant anything, that if any were to be disenfranchised it was those who could afford to wait, and not those who had waited so long. (Cheers.) He only wished the gentlemen who had brought forward the resolution would make it as good as their speeches, and that would be done by substituting the word "manhood" for "real."

Mr. Shaw, from the Tower Hamlets [John Shaw who had been imprisoned in Newgate] seconded the amendment. He observed that, though the Chartists were supposed dormant, their spirit still remained.

Nevertheless, there was considerable opposition to Bezer's amendment. George Jacob Holyoake urged its withdrawal, saying that whilst his friends said they did not come there to make division, they did make divisions. (Great clamour.) He also objected to the word "Manhood" suffrage, when it should also include womanhood suffrage.

Another speaker, on hearing that it was proposed to give votes to the army, asked how the working-men would like to be served as the men on the other side of the Channel had been? Following further discussion and a show of hands the chairman declared the amendment negatived.

This opposition by Holyoake to his proposed amendment induced Bezer to write a letter to Harney in the 13 March issue of the *Friend of the People*:

THE CHARTIST EXECUTIVE
To the Editor of the FRIEND OF THE PEOPLE.

SIR—May I be allowed a word to the members of the National Charter Association in your excellent paper?

It appears to me that an Executive who cannot act together, whose members oppose each other on material points, must burden the Chartist cause.

Mr. Holyoake and I are opposed; that gentleman's speeches, both at the Conference of the National Parliamentary Reform Association, and at the Aggregate Meeting at St. Martin's Hall, this week, did not, I think, represent the views of the majority of the members of the Chartist Association. I may be wrong, but both cannot be right, and as disunity in the Executive must increase disunity among the members, one of us ought to withdraw. Brother Chartists, which is it to be?

I am, your earnestly,
John James Bezer.

183, Fleet Street.

This observation by Bezer had also been made by Gerald Massey, and was becoming obvious to all. It was finally acknowledged at a meeting of the National Charter Association on the 24 March, when it was admitted that it was:

> The Executive of a society almost without members, and without means - members reduced to unwise antagonism without, and influence reduced by repeated resignations within... (*Reynolds' Weekly Newspaper*).

The last two mentions of Bezer in newspaper reports that year was by the *Star of Freedom* on the 12 and 19 June 1852. On the 12 June he is listed, amongst others, as giving 2/6d as a subscription to complete the payment of the NCA debt. On the 19 June he gave another small amount on behalf of the City Western locality.

About early July 1852, Bezer (as Publisher) was given (another account said he asked for) a cheque by Lord Goderich (George Robinson) the *Christian Socialist* supporter, in aid of the declining radical publication, the *Star of Freedom*. The Star's editor, George Julian Harney, not having received the money, made enquiries via Goderich, who learned that Bezer had fled to Australia in an emigration ship, leaving his wife behind. Prior to this, Bezer had been officially accepting money orders from subscriptions to the *Star of Freedom* made payable to him at the Strand Post Office (*Star of Freedom*, 26 June, 1852). However, there was no indication of any impropriety in those dealings.

Gerald Massey was so disgusted at such behaviour by a previous valued upholder of Chartist and Co-operative principles, that he sent an emotive over-coloured optimistic five verse poem encapsulating his opinions on the subject to Harney, for publication in the *Star of Freedom*:

THE DESERTER FROM DEMOCRACY.*

Another gone back, when our battle went sorest!
 Another soul sunk, like a star from the night!
Another hope quencht when our progress was poorest!
 Another barque wreckt, with the haven in sight!
Our Brother once - Traitor now: Nay, we'll not curse him,
 O Freedom forgive him, he knew not the cost!
He needeth our prayers, and if tears may amerce him,
 Then tears that are worlds of love, weep for the Lost!

Oh! little we thought when we tenderly bound him

Up, bleeding and torn from the fierce thorns of Life.
How all the sweet tendrils of love we twined round him,
   Would come home to die with such heartache and strife!
He thinks to flee from us?   God pity his blindness!
   For, we shall be near when, in Memory start
The old looks of Love, and the old voice of Kindness,
   He'll weep tears of blood yet; and eat his own heart!

He is gone from us!   Yet, shall we march on victorious;
   Hearts burning like Beacons - eyes fixt on the Goal -
And if we fall fighting, we fall like the Glorious
   With face to the stars; and all heaven in the soul!
And aye, for the brave stir of battle, we'll barter
   The sword of Life sheath'd in the peace of the grave
And better the radiant fire-robe of the Martyr,
   Than purple and gold of the glistering Slave!

He is gone!   Better so.   We should know who stand under
   Our Banner: let none but the trusty remain:
For there's stern work at hand, and the time comes shall
     sunder
   The shell from the pearl, and the husk from the grain.
And the Soul that thru danger and death will be dutiful,
   Chivalry's zeal, Martyr-faith, Hero-hands,
With pure heart, like a palace-home built for the Beautiful,
   Freedom of all her true lovers demands.

Lo! the Harvest bends rich for death!   Earth's long-Accurst
   Are ripe for Wrath's wine-press.   Sound Tyranny's knell!
For the heart of old Europe doth biggen and burst
   To hurry them into their own fiery Hell.
And the Lowly, with ear to the earth, catch the humming
   Of Freedom's Car-wheels, as they roll down the Time -
Which doth darken too flash forth the Glory that's coming
   To crown the old Cause with its triumph sublime.
                       GERALD MASSEY.
 * Alias, that blasted Bezer!

Harney did not publish the poem, but Massey included it, shortened and amended, in later editions of his poetical works.

In 1859, on the 12 October, Bezer's daughter, Emily Drew Bezer was baptised at St. Leonard's Church, Shoreditch. Parents named as:

John James Bezer, and Jane Sarah Bezer, residing at 9 Orchard Place, Shoreditch. Bezer's occupation, Cordwainer.

Orchard Place has not been found on available maps. It was probably within the area N.E. of Finsbury Circus, now redeveloped. Charles Booth (1898) notes it then as being entered from a crooked passage. Clean, but poor.

From the above information, there remains the question regarding Bezer's apparent reappearance.

1861

In census records of 1861, one of his sons is listed at:
6, Lower Felix Street, Bethnal Green.
Francis James Bezer, head, 23, Cordwainer. Born London, St Andrews.

Felix Street was sited between the east end of Hackney Road and Old Bethnal Green Road. It was continued as Lower Felix Street for a short distance. The area has been redeveloped as the Minerva Estate, at the corner of Hackney Road and Cambridge Heath Road.

Also from 1861:

3B Virginia Row, Bethnal Green.
Mary Nelson Bezer (Bezer's daughter), *14, apprentice, born Middlesex, London.*
Henry Thompson, head, 28, Machine Boot Closer [A person who sews the uppers of boots. Ed.]. Born Middlesex, Shoreditch.
Hannah Thompson, wife, 38, employing 2 women, born Wilts, Bradford.
Annie Thompson, daughter, 1, born Middlesex, Bethnal Green.

Virginia Row was situated in the area of the present Virginia Street, between Bethnal Green Road, Shoreditch High Street and Hackney Road.

This next extract also from the 1861 census is of interest:

2A Old Bethnal Green Road.
John Bezer, Head, 44 [enumerator's mark partly obscures].
Shoe Maker. Born Marthan, Norfolk.
Jane Bezer, Wife, 45. Boot Binder. Born Shoreditch, Middlesex.
Emily Bezer, daughter, 17, Fitter. Born Cripplegate, City of London.
Walter Bezer, son, 12, Scholar. Born Coleman Street, City of London.

But is the entry for John Bezer correct?

1862

Marriage. It was now the turn of Bezer's son, Francis James to get married. In November that year he married Emma Mander, 23, of John Street, at St James' Church, Shoreditch. He gave his details as a Bookseller, living at 2, William Street. His father, John James Bezer, named as a 'Publisher'. **A witness was Bezer's wife, Jane Sarah Bezer**.

William Street and John Street were both off Cannon Street, between Whitechapel Road and Cable Street. Now redeveloped.

1865

Marriage. Bezer's daughter Mary Nelson Bezer - previously noted as an apprentice - was married on 16 April at the Parish Church, Bethnal Green. Details given as a spinster, minor, of 22 Coleharbour Street, Bethnal Green. Father, John James Bezer, Stationer. She married George Frederick Fall, a bachelor and shoemaker, of 29 Henrietta Street, Bethnal Green.

Coleharbour (Coldharbour) Street and Henrietta Street not marked on available maps, but were in the area between Hackney Road and Old Bethnal Green Road.

1868

Marriage. At St. James' Church, Shoreditch, 1 March 1868: Bezer's last daughter, Emily Drew Bezer, 24, a Servant of 2 Holywell Row, married John Coe, 29, (of same address) a Leather Seller's Assistant. **John James Bezer, Publisher, stated then as Deceased**.

Holywell Row is between Shoreditch High Street and City Road.

1871

Mary Nelson Fall (Bezer) and family were living with an 8 month son at 29 Church Row, Wandsworth.

John Coe (Leather Seller), Emily Coe (Bezer) with son Francis F. Coe, now living at 84 Nuffield Road, Tower Hamlets.

1875

Marriage. Walter Cooper Bezer, Occupation 'Collector', married Caroline Mackenzie on 25 January 1875 at St Stephen, Bow, Middlesex. John James Bezer's occupation given as a 'Newsagent'.

1881

At the time of this census, Walter C. Bezer with his wife, Caroline, daughter Annie, 1, and Harriet Mackenzie, 32, sister-in-law (an unemployed domestic servant) were living then at 6 Cedar Mews, Clapham.

John Coe and wife Emily (Bezer), with Francis 12, and Hilda 6, were at 24 Odessa Road, West Ham.

1891

George Fall and Mary Nelson Fall (Bezer) had moved to Alpha Cottage, Tovells Road, Ipswich, now with 3 daughters and 3 sons.

As mentioned previously, according to Lord Goderich, Bezer had fled to Australia, [probably in early July 1852] after being given a cheque by Lord Goderich to help the *Star of Freedom*. Harney had written to Goderich, asking what he had done with Bezer, not having received the cheque. Mrs Bezer had also written, wanting to know what had become of her husband. John Ludlow commented that he 'levanted' to Australia with another man's wife, leaving his accounts in disorder. In addition, as a publisher, he had not submitted the required copies of the *Christian Socialist* to the British Museum Library or other institutions. In Australia, Ludlow stated, he 'went from bad to worse.'

Goderich soon had another occasion to express his displeasure with Bezer. Goderich was anxious to obtain a Liberal parliamentary position at Hull, but because of his Chartist and Christian Socialist sympathies, he found himself strongly opposed by the Hull Tories. With the help of Bezer and other workers who rallied the ships' carpenters and engineers, Goderich was elected on the 8 July 1852. During the election campaign, Goderich had wondered about some of the methods that had been used, and demand for money made, by his agents. After Bezer's disappearance, the Hull Tories found that some dubious transactions had taken place, and made official complaints, thus involving Goderich. However, following a petition and a House of Commons Select Committee Enquiry, the Committee fortunately acquitted Goderich of any personal wrongdoing and knowledge of the unethical activities of his agents.

Had Bezer disappeared due to receiving Goderich's money? Alternatively, because of his implication with the underhand methods used during the election campaign and fearing more time in prison, or perhaps both? From the last mention of him in 1868 – if correct - it might be assumed that John James Bezer had died between April/November 1862 and March 1868, but no British death certificate has been traced, or later census entries found for him or his wife. The father's name and occupation as given on later documents need not necessarily give the state of 'deceased'.

To Victoria and South Australia the emigration has continued to be conducted on the same principles as in former years. But in New South Wales a new principle has been introduced of great importance, and which, if it succeeds, will operate a considerable change in the position of the emigrants selected and sent out by this Board. The object of this change is to make the emigration to a great extent self-supporting. With this view the price of passage to a first-class emigrant is fixed at 13l., and to a second-class at 15l., and these amounts are required to be paid by or on account of each emigrant either in this country or in the colony. The proportion to be paid before embarkation and after arrival varies according to the age of the individual. Thus a first-class emigrant is required to pay :—

	Before embarkation.	After arrival.
If under 45 years of age	£1	£12
If over 45 and under 50	5	8
If over 50	11	2

A second-class emigrant is in like manner required to pay :

	Before embarkation.	After arrival.
If under 45 years of age	5	10
If over 45 and under 50	8	7
Over 50	15	—

No payments, however, are required either in this country or in the colony from the wives or children under 14, of emigrants sent out under this scheme.

From Emigration Commission Report, 1854

References

Charles Booth's notes for his *Life and Labour of the People of London*, a selection digitised – and online – by the London School of Economics.

Christian Socialist Vols I, II.

Harney Papers, ed. Black & Black, Assen, 1969.

John Ludlow. The Autobiography of a Christian Socialist, ed. A. Murray, London, 1981.

Life of the First Marquess of Ripon, by Lucien Wolf, London, 1921.

Northern Star, 23 September, 1848. Trial of the Chartist Prisoners.

Northern Star, 27 April, 1850. Meeting at the South London Chartist Hall.

The Northern Star also has short references during Bezer's political period.

Reynolds' Weekly Newspaper as cited.

Star of Freedom as cited.

Times as cited.

See also the biography of Gerald Massey.

4.

THE AUTOBIOGRAPHY OF ONE OF THE CHARTIST REBELS OF 1848
(From *The Christian Socialist* 1851)

[John James Bezer]

"And every one that was in distress, and every one that was in debt,
and every one that was discontented, gathered themselves unto him."

1 Samuel, xxii, v. 3

THE PAST.

"Let those who have in Fortune's lap
    Been softly nursed, repine
At days of childhood past and gone, -
    Their sorrows are not mine.

Let those whose boyish days were free
    From every ill and care,
Regret their flight, in pensive mood, -
    Their grief I cannot share.

Let those whose youth in pleasant years,
    Untroubled, swift, went by;
With aching heart sigh for the past, -
    With them I cannot sigh.

Let those whom now, in manhood's prime,
    No cares of peace bereave,
Lament the rapid pace of time, -
    With them I cannot grieve.

The retrospect of childhood's years,
    To me no pleasure brings;
Nor are my thoughts of boyish days
    The thoughts of pleasant things.
My youth was crossed, nor on my prime
    Does better fortune shine;
Then why should such a luckless wight
    O'er the dull past repine?

No! speed thee time - speed on, speed on!
    Thy haste I would not slack;
Still less, believe me, honest friend,
    I wish to see thee back.

Speed on - speed on then, to thy goal,
    And still with swifter wing!
From me thou can'st take nought away,
    Whatever thou mayst bring."

---

(1)

THE BIRTH

"A Chartist Rebel permitted to write in the *Christian Socialist*! I'll not take in another num."

" Hold, 'Tory Bill,' say nothing rashly."

"What *do* poor people want? Isn't there a prison for those who *do* grumble, and a workhouse for those who *don't*, with a Bible and Prayer-book in both places; and a Protestant (we'll have no Popery there) - a Protestant Chaplain to explain the texts properly, in order that they may know their duty to their superiors, and learn meekly to bow to all those placed in authority over them. *Can* the rich do more?"

"Yes. They can 'do unto others as they would be done unto.' They can 'sell (hard saying) *all* they have and follow Christ.' They can glorify God, and 'let his will be done on earth, as it is done in heaven.' They can confess (out of church as well as in it) 'that they have done that which they ought not to have done' - own that 'the earth is the Lord's, and the fulness thereof.' Shake hands with the poor, and

'Brothers be for a' that.' "

"Is there anything remarkable then in your life?"

"No, not very; except, perhaps, the Newgate affair - it is the life of millions in this 'happy land,' 'the admiration of the world, and the *envy* of surrounding nations' - where glorious Commerce has reached such perfection that everything, even the blood, and sweat, and lives, of white slaves, is bought cheap and sold dear, - so dear that the average lives of the poor in some towns amount to about seventeen years."

"Oh, I see it all now! You had *nought* to *lose* in 1848, and so your motto was, 'Down with everything, and up with nothing but anarchy, confusion, and civil war.' Thank God, however, and the *Special Constables*, the 10th of April showed."

"Showed what? - that class had arisen against class, where there ought to be no classes; that the lower orders had to wait a little longer; that there was a great gulf fixed between the poor and the rich which nothing but practical - mark! practical Christian Socialism can remove."

"Pooh, pooh - there must be always poor - the Lord ordained it - it is His will; - besides, the rich are very charitable - very; good Dukes of Cambridges everywhere; and this is a fine country after all - full of soup kitchens and straw-yards for the deserving poor; but they are never satisfied."

Between the hours of eleven and twelve on the morning of Saturday, 24th August, 1816, in Hope-street, Spitalfields, stood a little barber's shop, serving for parlour, kitchen and bedroom as well.

"They tells me as how you shaves here for a penny," said a patron of competition, who had been operated upon aforetime at the shop over the way for three halfpence.

"Yes, sir, I does," was the bland reply.

The man, after being barberously used, - paid, was thanked, and the penny - the first that day - placed on the mantle-shelf by the proprietor of the establishment with a sigh; in five minutes after, the Chartist Rebel was born in that self-same shop, with that solitary penny between the *three* of us, and the *brokers* in the place for six weeks' rent at 4s. per week! Strange to tell, mother and father were both confined on the same day - the former with a surplus population of one, the reward of twenty years' matrimonial love, - the latter with a drunken man in a dirty little watch-house, at the corner of Spitalfields' Church, the reward of knocking down the broker's man, - father considering in a moment of passion, that he was a surplus population of one in such an eventful hour as that. [Watch houses were built in the early 1800's, usually by the side of a church, to protect against grave-robbers. The police used them also to hold suspects for questioning, or to detain them until seen by a magistrate. Ed.]

"All's well however that *ends* well." Father was *up* and *out* again in a few hours, (as well as could be expected, as the ladies say), five shillings were borrowed from a cousin in White's Row, and never paid, I believe, (but I can plead the Statute of Limitations; besides I was a *minor* then), and better still, the landlord forgave us the rent, saying it was all through me. Thus was I worth to my parents, the first day I made a noise in the world, the sum of £1. 4s, sterling. So it proved "good tidings of comfort and joy" after all. My *ungrateful* parents have often told me that I was worth more to them on that day than I have been worth to them ever since.

Christ Church Spitalfields, where Bezer was confirmed 15 September 1816

I can assure my readers that the fact of the goods and chattels being seized upon made no effect on me, - nay, it would have made none even if I had been seized upon myself; so that mammy had been seized with me I should not have minded, the little I wanted I had, and if I could have sung, I should have chanted:

"I am content - I do not care,
Wag as it will the world for me."

Six months after my birth, my left eye left me for ever, - the small pox, the cause. For two months I was totally blind, and very bad, the "faculty" giving me over for dead more than once. The "faculty" were wrong; I recovered, minus an eye, and often have I been nearly run over through having a "single eye" towards the road; and often have I knocked against a dead wall, and hugged it as if I really loved the dark side of a question. Ah, I've had many a blow through giving half a look at a thing! How many times since I became a costermonger has a policeman hallooed in my ear, "Come! move hon there, vill yer! now go hon, move yer hoff!" while I've actually thought he was on duty in some kitchen with the servant girl, taking care of the house as the master and mistress were out. It was not however so; there he has stood in all his beauty, a Sir Robert Peel's monument - a real one, alive, - and sometimes have I seen him *kicking*.

(2)

THE SUNDAY SCHOOL*

"Then he got eddication,
Just fit for his station,
For yer knows we all on us a summet must larn."
Mister Benjamin Block.

Right, "Ben," but *what*? Shall it tend to good or ill? A most important question, that not only infinitely concerns the neglected victims of a bad or insufficient education, but society at large; evil training, sir, is like the measles - catching! he who commits a bad action has generally learned to do so, and then he learns another, and so the disease goes on.

My education was very meagre; I learnt more in Newgate than at my Sunday school, but let me not anticipate.

Among the many days I shall probably for life remember, is the 21st of December, 1821, when breeched for the first time, and twopence in my bran-new pocket, I proudly marched to Raven Row Sunday School and had my name entered. From that hour, until the hour I finally left, which, with the exception of two intervenings of short duration, lasted nearly fifteen years, I can truly say I loved my school, - no crying when Sunday came round.

"I loved that blessed day
The best of all the seven."

I yearned for it; whether it was because my home was not as it ought to have been, (a painful subject I shall feel bound to say something about in due order,) or because association has ever seemed dear to me, or because I desired to show myself off as an apt scholar, or because I really wanted to learn, or all these causes combined - most certainly I was ever the first to get in to school, and the last to go out.

I ought to have learned a great deal, say you, in fifteen years; well, in the opinion of some, I did, for notwithstanding the disadvantages I laboured under both at home and at school, and there only being six hours a week for me, I rapidly rose from class to class; at seven years old I was in the "testament class" - at eight, in the highest - shortly after, "head boy" - soon after that, "monitor" - at eleven, teacher - and long before I left, head teacher; - and yet, what had I learned? To read well, and that was all. Three years ago I knew nothing of arithmetic, and could scarcely write my own name.

I have just spoken of the disadvantages at school - I shall doubtless displease some of my readers in what I am going to say, but when I commenced this history, I determined that it should be a genuine one, and that I would put down my thoughts without reserve. Now, that school did not even learn me to read; six hours a week, certainly not one hour of useful knowledge; plenty of cant, and what my teachers used to call explaining difficult texts in the Bible, but little, very little else.

I am not going to enter into any theological discussion, but I am going to tell the discipline, routine, and teaching of an average London Dissenting Sunday School of a quarter of a century ago.

'Tis nine o'clock, Sabbath-day morning, the girls and the boys, old and young, are promiscuously mingling together on the door steps; about a quarter past, the teachers begin to arrive, and the doors are opened - a rush up stairs, and a little order restored by the superintendent going round with the early attendance reward tickets, taking at least another quarter of an hour, - then a hymn sung, very likely the following:

> "Not more than others I deserve,
> *Yet* God hath given me more."

And worse still –

> "For *I* have food, while *others* starve,
> And beg from door to door."

Now, I would rather believe in no God at all, than in such a one as is described in this verse. What! praise the Great Supreme Being, who is no respecter of persons, for giving me plenty to eat, and causing others at least as good as I, to starve though surrounded with plenty; rank blasphemy! it is such teaching as this, that keeps up our monster social evils, from generation to generation, the young mind is taught to attribute that to God, which only "Man's inhumanity to man" has brought about.

However, I used to sing it most lustily, though sometimes hungry myself, - and so did my fellow scholars, whether hungry or full deponent is not able to say. Well then, after the singing, an extempore prayer by one of the teachers in turn - a prayer, the language and meaning of which few children could, or desired to understand. At last, about ten, the classes are arranged only to be disarranged at half-past, that being chapel time. Afternoon at two, the same manner of "teaching the young idea how to shoot," till near three, - the classes are arranged again, and the teacher (probably not the one who taught in the morning) commences to teach, and what does he teach? It is an A B C class, say, composed of twelve tiny little boys, number one says in a drawling dying tone, "*hay*," number two, "*be-e*," and so on, till some one makes a blunder, and then he's sent last, his blunder *sometimes* sharpening the wits of the rest, but more frequently causing jealousy and in some instances, (I have known them myself,) lasting hatred. Even this secular education, bad as it was, did not last above half an hour. The teacher would tell us to shut up our books, and talk to us about hell-fire, and eternal brimstone, and how wicked we was, and if we didn't believe all he said to us, we should be burnt for ever and ever, which of course made us feel very comfortable till four, - then another hymn, and an address delivered from the desk to all the children, the orator dwelling on some theological dogma, giving his own peculiar views in an exceedingly peculiar manner - a prayer - a rush out, and all was ended for a week.

I ask, is such education as this worth having? Is it suitable? Is it that sort of "milk for babes," calculated to nourish and strengthen, and elevate the growing man, who *will* grow for better or for worse. You inquire, perhaps, "Would I advocate a purely secular education?" I cannot say I would. I would inculcate the being of a God - a God of justice - of love - of mercy; more - I would impress on the young mind, that this world of ours was a probationary state, that they that *done* evil were punished here and hereafter, and they that *done* good, their reward was with them, and future glory in another and better world than this; but beyond this, I would no further go; all else I would leave entirely with the parents, and their respective ministers, every creed standing on its own foundation, without help or hindrance from the state.

[* On this theme, see John Critchley Prince, *The Sunday School*.]

(3)

MY FATHER AND MY HOME

"A crust of bread, a bed of straw, and rags."
Hood.

Father kept a barber's shop, trade was brisk, and times much better than they are now, so that when he really *did* attend to his business; he cleared a good round sum weekly. Mother also earned at cotton winding (before machinery, or rather the monopoly of machinery altered it,) nine or ten shillings weekly; yet there we were, miserably poor, and the quotation at the head of this chapter was literally my experience for years during my childhood, except a few short months that I remained with my aunt, who, though well off, treated me shamefully, and I ran home again, that being the lesser evil.

Father was a drunkard, a great spendthrift, an awful reprobate. Home was often like a hell; and "Quarter days" - the days father received a small pension from Government for losing an eye in the Naval Service - were the days mother and I always dreaded most; instead of receiving little extra comforts, we received extra big thumps, for the drink maddened him. The spirit of the departed will pardon, and, I verily believe, will rejoice at my speaking thus plainly, not only because it is the truth, but in order to show, as I shall show, the power of Christian principles as exemplified in the after life of him who was as a "brand plucked from the burning."

Father had been an old "man-o'-wars man," and the many floggings he had received while serving his country, had left their marks on his back thirty years afterwards; they had done more, - they had left their marks on his soul. They had unmanned him; can you wonder at that? Brutally used, he became a brute - an almost natural consequence; and yet there are men to be found even to this day, advocates of the lacerating the flesh and hardening the hearts of their fellow creatures simultaneously.

The loss of a considerable sum of money by my father while at sea through the chicanery of his sister, tended, I doubt not, to increase his love for drink. Church or chapel was never thought of by him from his youth till he was upwards of fifty years of age; then - but I will give the facts without comment.

The late Mr. Isaacs, of Gloster Chapel, Hackney, used to lecture on Tuesday evenings, at the time I am speaking of, at Staining Lane Chapel, City. This gentleman was a favourite minister with my mother, and she was constantly begging father to go and hear him, without avail; she would always get ridiculed for her pains, till Tuesday evening, November 15, 1823, I think, - on that night he offered himself to go if mother would treat him to some gin. She did, and we all three went; father scoffing and swearing, and mother, I doubt not, inwardly praying on our journey. The service had commenced; indeed, the text - the 40th Psalm, 1st verse ("I waited patiently for the Lord, and he inclined unto me and heard my cry") - was just being read as we entered. Presently I noticed, child as I was, the altered looks of father, and as the minister seemed to increase in energy and zeal, father literally trembled again, so much so that several of the congregation noticed it. At length the service ended, and directly we got out, father said,

"Mary, my dear," - the first kind words I had heard him utter for years –
"Mary, my dear, let us go home. God have mercy upon me, a miserable sinner."

Not a word else, to my recollection, escaped him that night. We all kept awake, for the scene appeared to my young mind terrible. The agony of father was indescribable for several days.

At last, without any visitor coming to him, but solely through reading the Bible, hope dawned upon him, and from that time till he died, above eight years, he was a changed man - no more drunkenness or immorality. At the expense of being laughed at, and called a canter, as I know I shall be by some who read this, I cannot refrain from giving a few lines from a hymn he never seemed tired of singing, because they exactly portray his altered character and feelings: -

"These eyes that once abused their sight
Now lift to Thee their watery light
        And weep a silent flood."
                *   *   *
"These ears that once could entertain
The midnight oath, the lustful strain,
        Around the festal board, -
Now deaf to all the enchanting noise,
Avoid the throng, detest the joys,
        And press to hear Thy word."

The consequences, however, of this remarkable change in my father did not better our pecuniary circumstances. This may appear strange, but it is easily explained. My father's conscientious convictions would not allow him to open his shop on Sundays, and as it was a very poor neighbourhood, Sunday was better than all the week beside to him. His customers rapidly fell off because he was not such "a jolly good fellow" as he was wont to be. All called him mad, the *publicans* especially condemning him as a matter of course; his constitution, too, was so much injured by drink, that the sudden change to strict sobriety seemed utterly to prostrate him, and he was always ill. Mother's work also got slack and worse paid. Still they persevered, and still things got worse, and though "a dry morsel with quietness" was a glorious improvement on the past, they could not at last meet the expenses of the veriest necessities of life. The climax to all was, that the Government pension was stopped altogether, in consequence of father petitioning for an increase, the authorities offering him the hospital. Our little home, which though humble, had become precious to us, was broken up, the persecuted saint went to Greenwich College, and mother and I became out-door paupers to a parish in the City that father claimed through his apprenticeship.

"All these things were against us," except that they made a lasting impression on my youthful mind, and I stuck to my Sunday school and to my faith with all the fervour and enthusiasm God had given me.

Greenwich Hospital and Royal Naval Asylum, south aspect, c. 1800

Greenwich College was the Old Royal Naval College - Greenwich Hospital - a residential home with accomodation at its peak for some 2,500 injured and disabled sailors. The Royal Naval Asylum for children of seamen was closed in 1821. The Old Royal Naval College was closed in 1869 due to declining numbers and was taken over by the Royal Naval College in 1873, eventually becoming a Royal Naval Training Establishment.

MY FIRST EMPLOYMENT

The parish allowed us four shillings weekly, and with that miserable stipend, and about two shillings more for cotton winding, we managed to pay rent and buy bread till the near approach of Easter in the next year; *then* we bought buns - not for the purpose of eating, (though we did eat them after all), but for the purpose of selling again. Three shillings and one little basket were borrowed for this important occasion: - mother put two shillings' worth of buns in the basket, and one shilling's worth in the tea-tray for me, and off we trudged different ways. Mother had given me my round, but then it was much nearer home and Sunday school than I cared about, and worse still, it was a leading thoroughfare. Did I want people to see me? No. - "if people couldn't buy buns without seeing the seller, it was strange," so with aching heart, and scalding tears, and scarlet face, I walked up and down the most by-streets, and *whispered* so low that nobody could hear me,

"Hot cross buns!
One a penny, two a penny, hot cross buns,"

till, all the gods of Homer will bear me witness, they were as *cold* as the corpse of a Laplander; still I called them *hot* from seven till twelve, and took the magnificent sum of Twopence! ... Philosophers talk of never giving up, - I think it was Charles II. who said, after reading the following epitaph on a tombstone,

This man never knew fear

"then he never snuffed a candle with his fingers" - and I say to any philosopher of *nine years old*, - cry hot cross buns for the first time, for five hours, till you are as cold as they are, and hungry enough to eat the "stock," and then if you don't talk of giving up, you are a noble little fellow.

I went home - folks had laughed at me, had rejoiced when I wept, but only two persons had bought. I went home, I say, determined most dutifully to present mother with the remains of my merchandise, thinking, of course, she had sold out, and would be ready to sell mine too, when lo! my venerable and courageous parent had sold none at all; having met a person she had known years before when she was better off, her courage failed, and she came home again almost directly, and had been looking for me all round the neighbourhood. To tell you the real truth, reader, I was right glad of this, spite of our desperate circumstances - it prevented her finding fault with me; so after we had had our soiree of tea and buns, mother moved, and I seconded, a resolution, to the effect that we would never go out with buns any more, hot or cold. But then what was to be done?

"I'll get a place," said I.

"You, boy! So young and so ailing?"

"I will;" and so I did the very next Monday. May God forgive my tyrant master for the acute sufferings I then endured...

"If you please, Sir, do you want a boy? My name is ----- ; mother winds cotton for you, sir; father is in Greenwich College, and we are in great distress - almost starving, sir; I'll be very willing to do anything."

"Why, you're so little! What's your age?"

"Past nine, sir, and I'm *very* strong!"

"What wages do you want?"

"Anything you please, sir." (The healthy competition was all one side.)

"Well, come to-morrow morning, six o-clock, and if you suit I'll give you three shillings a-week; but bring all your victuals with you - we have no time for you to go home to your meals."

Thus was I duly installed at a Warehouseman's in Newgate Street.

Black slavery is black enough, I doubt not, and white slavery is a very horrid thing in all its ramifications, for it has many - the factory children, and so on; - there is pity, however, manifested towards these unfortunates, and sometimes help, but who ever thought of errand-boy slavery?

"Willing to do anything."

Yes, and *anything* I did, - wait in the cold and sleet for half-an-hour each morning at master's street door - clean a box full of knives and forks, a host of boots and shoes in a damp freezing cellar - gulp down my breakfast, consisting of a hunk of bread, *perhaps* buttered, and a bason of water bewitched, called tea, in the cold warehouse - run to Whitechapel with a load they called a parcel - back again.

"John, make haste to Piccadilly with this."
Back again.

"John, your mistress wants you to rub up the fire-irons and candlesticks, and clean the house windows."

"John, look sharp, and have your dinner, you're wanted to go over the water with a lot of things."

(Dinner! God help me! A penny saveloy when it was not in the dog days, and a "penn'orth of baked plain" when it was, or bread alone at the latter end of the week) - trail along with my bag full of "orders" along Blackfriars, Walworth, London Road, City, and back to Newgate Street.

"John, look alive, ---- of Islington Green, wants this parcel directly."
Back again.

"Now, John, all the 'orders' are ready for the West, so as soon as you've had your tea (tea!), you can start; you needn't come back here to-night, - bring the bag in the morning."

Though master *said* my time was from six to eight, yet it was always half-past seven, sometimes later, ere I could start to the "West," which meant haberdashers shops up Holborn, Soho, Oxford Street, Regent Street, Piccadilly, over Westminster Bridge to two shops near the "Broadway," and *then*, eleven o'clock at the earliest, trudge home to Spitalfields, foot-sore and ready to faint from low diet and excessive toil, and this, too, for years without one day's intervention save Sundays, for my master was religious of course. Every night would I crawl home with my boots in my hand, putting them on again before I got in, trying to laugh it off while I sank on my hard bed saying,

"Never mind mother, I don't mind it, you know I'm getting bigger every day."

Indeed 'tis hard:

"To smile when one would wish to weep,
To speak when one would silent be,
To wake when one would wish to sleep,
And wake to agony."

Certainly I could have left my place, for this is a free country. What then, should I have got another? And if I had, that's not all - my master was my mother's master; and if I had discharged myself, he would have discharged her; he has told me so often - which of course is free trade - so I toiled on, for father was as it were dead to me, and mother always ailing, and I saw no alternative but the workhouse, that worst of all prisons so dreaded by the poor, - so I toiled on, I say, till I was about eleven years of age; then typhus fever laid me prostrate, and for weeks I was to all appearance dying. I was glad to hear that the parish doctor gave me up, and the farewell of my teachers and my fellow Sunday scholars I loved so well, and my poor dear father who crawled on crutches to see me, was, though affecting, happiness to me. I felt an ardent desire for death - but it was not to be. I at last recovered. Still was I thankful even for my illness, inasmuch as it gave me a respite from

"Iscariot Ingots Esquire,
That highly respectable man."

SIGNS OF REBELLION

My Master was continually inquiring after my health, though he gave not a sixpence towards improving it; but when I had sufficiently recovered, sent for me, and offered to take me back at 4s. a week instead of 3s., and give my mother full work besides, if I complied with his request. I did so, and the day after heard that five boys had discharged themselves during my three months' illness. I had to go through the same routine - endure the same bullying - but mother *did* get more work, (though at ld. a pound, the same as she got 4d. four years before, and 2d. for just before my illness, but then that was to make up, I dare say, for the extra 1s. he gave me).

Well, Father would come out of the College; he rallied somewhat, and went "a barbering" round Bethnal-green, a sort of itinerant shaver. The parish stopped the supplies immediately; but Father cleared about 6s. or 7s. - Mother about 3s. 6d., which, with my earnings, amounted to 13s. or 14s. per week; provisions were dearer then than they are at the present time, yet as we were very economical, not only did we manage necessaries, but our home became gradually more comfortable.

As winter, however, came on, Father's rheumatism - as bad an *ism* as a man can be plagued with, - I speak feelingly - laid him on his beam ends; and separation was again our fate. The "College" received him till he died. Mother, too, just at this time fell dangerously ill; and for many nights - hard as I worked in the day - I had no rest. God bless the poor! *they* saved her life when parish doctor, and parish overseer had passed her by, and said that the workhouse would take me, after they had buried Mother; - the poor neighbours - not the rich ones - played the part, as they always do, of good Samaritans, by rushing to the rescue, and nursing her in turns night and day for weeks, without fee, or thinking of fee. God bless the poor! Amen!

Master's tyranny became more and more insupportable. I will give the reader an instance. In the second week of Mother's illness, I was sent to Mile-end Road with a parcel, and as we then lived in High-street, Mile End New Town, close by, nature predominated over my fear of offending, and I came home; it was thought Mother would not live an hour. I stayed that hour, and yet she breathed - and I ran back with quick step but heavy heart.

"What has made you so long, sir?"

I told him the truth, and he kicked me! I never remember feeling so strong, either in mind or body, as I did at that degrading moment; I threw the day-book at him with all my might, and before he could recover his presence of mind, sprang on the counter, and was at his throat. I received some good hard knocks, which I returned, - if not with equal force, - with equal willingness, crying,

"Oh, if my poor Father were here," - "I'll tell Father" -"I'll go to the Lord Mayor" - "I'll tell everybody."

The tussle didn't last long, and the result was that we gave each other warning; and I, nothing daunted, threatened to stand outside the street door, and create a crowd by telling every one as they passed all about it; whilst he threatened, in his turn, to give me into custody for tearing his waistcoat and assaulting him, saying I should get into Newgate Closet before I died.

The spirit of prophecy must have manifested itself in a remarkable manner at that moment to that great man. For, lo! as he said, so it came to pass, though many years afterwards. I will not however, give him all the praise. The "signs of rebellion" were just then rather clear. I was, to all intents and purposes, a "physical force rebel," and I doubt not that "the coming event cast its shadow before" the mind's eye of the immortal W. that is to say, if the immortal W. *had* a mind.

The craven, on that day week, asked me to stay with him; I refused, except for a week longer; that same night, though, I "got the sack." It was past nine o'clock when I started for the West, and trailing up Holborn-hill with my bag full of orders nearly dragging the ground behind me, a policeman - a *new* policeman we called them then - stopped me:

"You sir, what er ye got in there, a?"

Now I was not in the best of humours just then; indeed, "Crushers" were never very popular with me; - so, (alluding to the policeman who had stolen a leg of mutton a while before, and which was all the talk), I answered promptly, looking at the gentleman as impudently as an embryo Chartist well could,

"Legs o' mutton."

"I'll leg o' mutton yer," says he; and off I was taken to the Station.

The Superintendent behaved very kindly to me, sending the policeman back with me to Master's, with the complimentary message, that "M. ought to know better than send so young a boy at so late an hour, with such a load, round the West-end, and that the 'Force' had strict orders to stop any one with loads after nine o'clock, so I had better go in the morning." Master at once gave me my wages, and ordered me not to come again, telling me at the same time that when Mother got better, she need not apply to him for work. But what think you? The next day he sent for me again, and I staid with him two months longer, for 5s. a-week, which, with the parish allowance, that had dropped to 3s. was all that we had.

Holborn Hill from the corner of Snow Hill, with Farringdon Street (then New Bridge Street Market) on the left and St Andrew's Church in the background.
ca. 1830

A view of Holborn Hill from opposite St Andrew's Church.
The entrance to Shoe Lane is on the left of the Church. ca. 1830

The Superintendent of my Sunday-school about this time offered me a place at 1s. a week and my victuals, and didn't I close in with the offer without hesitation! The word *victuals* decided me at once, for Mr. A. kept two Ham and Beef Shops, and the bare idea of becoming a "beef-eater" was so agreeable a novelty, that without a moment's warning to my Newgate-street master, I went to my new situation. I trust my vegetarian readers will pardon my backsliding; I had been compelled to luxuriate so long on vegetable *marrow*, that I confess it appeared no *marrow* to me, and I desired a change; besides, you know, I was led into temptation; - Ham and beef, after bread and potatoes! Oh! 'Twas a consummation devoutly to be wished!

I did not keep this good place, however, but about four months, and it was my own fault. The apprentice, who was also Master's nephew, was a wild animal of seventeen years old, and Mr. A. told me from the first, that I was to try and reclaim him.

"John, talk to him, I know you can, and though he is five years older than you, your example will shame him into reformation."

I *did* talk to him like a parson, at first, and acted as I talked; but alas, evil communications corrupt good manners. At last he influenced me, not I him; and though I cannot recollect committing any really immoral or dishonest act, I became very flighty and careless, and incurred the displeasure of my kind master, who at length discharged me, and served me right, for the following very *dirty* spree: - one day we had cooked an extra quantity of hams and rounds of beef, and *then* got into the coppers to swim, as the apprentice called it; he escaped without observation, but I staid enjoying myself, and floundering about in this novel bath for the people, till, who should come right into the cookery but mistress herself; it was all over with me; I implored for mercy but in vain. Master, with tears in his eyes, - he was a glorious soul - said that he wished he could discharge his nephew instead of me, but we must part; he gave me a most excellent character to my next place, a Chemist's, at the corner of Jewin-street, which I kept for near five years.

What happened there to me, my Christian experience during those five years, the effects the agitation for the "Reform Bill" had on my mind, &c., shall form the subject of my next chapter. What I have already written, and what I shall write for a little time, is not very interesting to the readers of this journal, I dare say - it is merely one of "the simple annals of the poor;" but as John Nicholls has it:

'It may perhaps, appear ridiculous to fill so much paper with babblings of one's self; but when a person who has never known any one interest themselves in him, who has existed as a *cipher* in society, is kindly asked to tell his own story, how he will gossip!'

Exactly so.

(6)

SACKCLOTH AND ASHES

I once clothed myself in sackcloth and ashes, *literally* so; and this is how it was, - attend, reader, while I explain, for, believe me, it is important. We had a library in our Sunday school; ah, we *just had such a library*, - "Drelincourt upon Death" with the lying ghost story attached, that Defoe forged, (little thinking, good soul, that it would be made a Sunday school Old Bogie of); then "Allen's" I think, or "Aleyn's" "Alarm to the Unconverted," and many others too, nearly all of the same stamp. But two bright stars in this black firmament we had - Nos. 85 and 86, I shall never forget the numbers, how many times have I read them - Bunyan's "Pilgrim's Progress," and Bunyan's "Holy War." - My own dear Bunyan! If it hadn't been for you, I should have gone mad, I think, before I was ten years old! Even as it was, the other books and teachings I was bored with, had such a terrible influence on me, that somehow or other, I was always nourishing the idea that "Giant Despair" had got hold of me, and that I should never get out of his "Doubting Castle." Yet I read, ay, and *fed* with such delight as I cannot *now* describe - though I think I could then. Glorious Bunyan, you too were a "Rebel," and I love you *doubly* for *that*. I read you in Newgate, - so I could, I understand, if I had been taken care of in Bedford jail, - your books are in the library of even your Bedford jail. Hurrah for progress! How true it is, that

"Even the wrong is proved to be wrong!"

I am digressing though; - let's see, we were talking of sackcloth and ashes.

My teacher, at the time I was speaking of, was an earnest gloomy soul who, if he delighted in anything, delighted in minutely describing the wrath to come; and he *could do it* well. How have I cried while listening to him, and how *pleased* he'd be at my tears, as if sorrow and religion were inseparable. One Sunday afternoon he was particularly eloquent on the anger and *vengeance* of God, and as a climax, told us about the men of old who went in "sackcloth and ashes," and whose "tears were gathered up in the Lord's bottle" (D---- was always very grand and *figurative* at *expounding*).

As I went home I felt dreadful, yet a beam of hope shone - oh, if I could only get the opportunity, nobody seeing me, of doing as the "*ancients*" did, I should be saved! So, begging of father and mother (I was not *nine years* old at the time) to let me stay in, while they went to chapel – I actually undressed myself to the skin, got out of the cupboard father's sawdust bag, wrapped myself in it, poured some ashes over my head, and stretched myself on the ground, imploring for mercy, with such mental agony and such loud cries that the people in the house heard me, and told my parents about it, though nobody even then knew the truth. Readers will doubtless laugh at this childish folly, - I marvel if some of them have not committed as fantastic tricks, if they would only own it!

One fellow-scholar I told this to a few years ago, and who is now an *infidel* through such teaching, admitted that he had done precisely the same. *Yes, through such teaching,* - and I know several such cases, - children have been brought to compare themselves to the Manasseh and the *"Chief"* of sinners, till the rebound in after years has led them to suppose that they are no sinners at all, and now they laugh at everything sacred, because everything sacred was mauled about and distorted to suit the views (views!) of anybody who unfortunately "had a call." They were told to believe in a God of *vengeance*, and worse still, *partiality*, and so now they believe in *no* God; they have been told that there were "children in hell not a span long," and rather than believe *that*, they have banished every idea of a future state altogether. It had nearly that effect on me. "High Calvinists," prepare to meet your God! your gloomy, blood-stained, fanatical teachings have been one of the principal causes of the spread of atheism among us. Oh, my dear fellow Sunday school teachers! We have done that which we ought not to have done – we have bent the twig the wrong way – it is we, not infidel, but *we* who have often "turned the truth of God into a lie", and made a creature of Him Who is the Creator. We have crippled the glorious image God had made, and *then* – horrible – *then* likened it to the imagemaker.

Of course I was "converted" as they call it – oh, to be sure! – and made head-boy of, because I was a "miserable sinner." and didn't I get promoted for it; and wasn't I monitor, and teacher – ay, *teacher* long before I was twelve years old, - and didn't I join the Church at sixteen, and was baptised, and called a "dear promising youth," one who was to be a "burning and a shining light," a minister in "god's own time," one of those "few champions for the truth" who would prove to all the world that nearly all the world was damned, and that the "elect precious" meant only our own precious selves? But now "I am an apostate," say you; am I? Judge not that ye be not judged. I am earnest in propagating that which I think to be truth now, and so I was then, but I did it ignorantly, and shall be forgiven.
One thing must not be omitted in these humble memoirs; and that is, to give my testimony against those persons who are so fond of saying,

that religious people *are* so because it is their interest, and that their zeal is in accordance with their pay. I must admit that there are many white-washed walls, many hypocrites; I could lay bare facts relative to the conduct of both ministers and people, black enough, God knoweth. What then? Such statements would only cause additional pain to conscientious men of all creeds, and serve no good purpose either. Besides, if we are to attack persons for principles, there is an end to all argument, - yet is the outward walk of professors, the first, the primary thing the poor unlettered men look at - no logic is so powerful with us as *that* - and if the outward walk be wrong, most of us jump to wrong conclusions.

I deny, however, most emphatically, and with long experience on my side, I deny, that the motives of Christian people, as a *rule*, are impure. Those who look after and get the "loaves and fishes" form the exception, and this exception is principally confined (will the Editor allow this sentence to be inserted?) to the parsons - indeed, *when they have dined*, there are nothing near twelve baskets' full of fragments remaining, *they'll take care of that*. In the Christian world or in the outer, both among the Dissenters and in the Church, those get the most pay who do the least work. There were always collections, monthly, quarterly, and annually, besides tea-meetings and other dodges, for the "dear minister" at the chapel I was a member of; and often have I gone hungry, and mother too, because we gave our very bread into the "plates" at the door, which the deacons on both sides thereof held so close to each other that they seemed to say, "No thoroughfare to Dissenters on the voluntary principle." Yet the "dear minister" didn't work a tenth part so hard as I did in the cause, - but then, mine was a "labour of love." Just as if preaching couldn't be a labour of love also; I see no reason why people couldn't make sermons and make tents too (especially as there's a surplus population of them - I mean parsons, not tents: just now) in 1851 as they did in 51. Perhaps, however, it's all through machinery.... At all events, I feel that I am now meddling with things too high for me, and that the bare suggestion is a kind of spiritual rebellion. You must pardon my egotism though, if I describe my Sabbath day's work:

'Tis a summer's Sunday morning. I rise at six o'clock, and get to Spital Square by seven, in order to commence the out-door services, which closed after eight; school just after nine, hard at it, arranging the classes (I was superintendent at this time), till chapel service, which I had to commence, being clerk - giving out the following hymn, perhaps,

"Well the Redeemer's gone
Before His Father's face,
To *sprinkle o'er the burning throne!*
And turn the wrath to grace!!"

(Reader, pause, and ask yourself solemnly the question, if this is a true, a reasonable, a scriptural picture of the unchangeable God, in Whom there is no variableness or shadow of turning, and Who is the same yesterday, to-day, and for ever.)

Well, chapel would not be over till one, and at halfpast, I'd be teaching a select singing-class; at two, school commenced again; at four, I would go out distributing tracts, if it wasn't my turn to deliver the address to the children, then at half-past four; this took me till evening service (often have I had my tea at Spitalfields' pump). Evening service closed, a prayer-meeting in a large room close by, at which I gave an address one Sunday, a fellow teacher composing the hymns suitable - he giving an address the next Sunday, and I composing the hymns that night for him, which, by-the-bye, as it was rather a novel thing, every hymn sung for upwards of a twelve-month being original, soon filled the place, and we could often boast of having a larger congregation than the minister of the chapel. I was never home till after ten at night. I did it without pecuniary reward, or dreaming of it, and this toil, for toil it was, though I did not think so then, lasted a considerable period.

7

A SLAP AT THE CHURCH

I have been requested by more than one valued friend to insert a few hymns and other compositions of my earlier years. There are several reasons for respectfully objecting, but two will very likely suffice. First, I can't, because but one is preserved; and secondly, I won't, because that one is not worth preserving. Indeed, if I am to go on jabbering at this rate, there'll be nobody to read the Rebel's Autobiography save the Rebel himself, and I want to get over that part relating to my religious experience as quickly as can well be, connecting it together at once, without referring again to the subject.

I have been a Churchman as well as a Dissenter, and the being a Churchman for a few months made me a Dissenter for ever. Mother was a Churchwoman according to Act of Parliament. The poor old body didn't perfectly comprehend the difference between a church that was established by law and a church that wasn't, and I have often thought that if others had, been as dark in their understandings on the matter as she was, there would have been much less malice, hatred, and all uncharitableness among us. But no; we have "perfectly comprehended" how to differ, forgetting - some of us, I fear, wilfully - that it would be much easier to agree. A good old minister once said:

There is Calvinist-street, and Baptist-street, and Wesleyan-street, and Independent street, and Church-street, and Dissent-street, all leading to the High Road, if we are but sincere, and we needn't jostle each other, though the streets are narrow.

That's it, *sincerity* –

"He can't be wrong whose life is in the right."

But then that's not orthodoxy. Well, its *my* doxy, and I am writing my auto., if you please. I protest against a great deal that is called Protestantism and Dissent from a great many Dissenters, yet must I have a "Slap at the Church." This phrase is borrowed. When I was errand-boy at the Doctor's, the agitation for the Reform Bill, the whole Bill, and - botheration to it - nothing but the Bill, was all the go. I well remember the bellman going round Cripplegate, announcing the majority of one, and the excitement created round the neighbourhood. Among the many periodicals living on the agitation, was one yclept "A Slap at the Church," - my master's favourite paper; for master was a great radical - one who'd beat his wife and shout for reform with all the enthusiasm of a glorious freeman; like many radicals in the present day, who can prate against tyranny wholesale and for exportation, and yet retail it out with all their hearts and souls, whenever they have an opportunity. Well, this "Slap at the Church" [a weekly illustrated periodical of 1832. Ed.] I'd con over in my leisure moments. I don't recollect what it contained, except that it was of a very meagre and abusive description; but I *do* recollect that there was always on the frontispiece a superior wood engraving of an exceedingly elevated character, most likely a Bishop, who was sure to be represented as enormously stout. I never had the honour of seeing but one Bishop in my life, but I have been taught both by oral and written traditions to believe, that to be a Bishop you *must* be a fat man; and so rooted and grounded was I in this faith, that when a Bishop who *happened* to be remarkably thin passed through Newgate Prison, while I was examining for a few months the place, I wouldn't believe it was one.

"He is indeed," said the Governor, "it is the Lord Bishop of ----."

"Then, sir," said I, "the Whigs have been starving not only the People but the Priests, and there *will* be a row, for they won't stand it."

In a former chapter it has been told you, that mother and I were paupers. Now mother, directly she got on the "books," was expected to attend her parish Church; I say expected, because that was the emphatic expression of the poor-law guardian, and all paupers know that when his worship the guardian *expects* a thing, he generally gets it. Moreover, there were some free seats *made on purpose for paupers*, so admirably constructed that most of the dearly-beloved rich brethren - separated of course by pews, in direct contradiction to the injunction of that uncouth Christian Socialist James - could see how their poorer brethren behaved themselves. An excellent arrangement, - else, there would have been nothing to look at but the clergyman, and nothing to hear but merely the gospel. If those seats hadn't been filled by a respectable number of non-respectable dependants on our free institutions, the awful spectacle of Fraternity would have been exhibited in all its revolutionary deformity in the very House of God - shocking! So, to obviate such infidelity as *that*, Twopenny Loaves - always of the same size - and Sixpence, were given away weekly to all who could claim the parish, and who couldn't claim a conscience. I was one of that number, - yes, for more than six months every Sunday morning, one of that number.

"B——, why don't your son come with you? You know he's on our books."

"I'll tell him, sir."

She knew how hard it was to get me away from my dear Sunday school. At last the order came, ay, the *order* - do you doubt my word? Do you tell me that this is England? I repeat, the *order*; tyrants can play their game by more moves than one - the order, in the shape of the following protestant inquisitorial mandate, given by the Right Honourable the Guardian, in the year of our Lord, 1828, in the city of London as aforesaid.

"Your boy *belongs* to us the same as yourself, and we shall expect him next Sunday; if he don't come, why, of course we can't *keep* two of you, that's all I got to say."

So I went - was ushered into the presence of the Rector, and examined in the most pompous manner imaginable,

"Do you know your Catechism?"

"Yes, Sir;" (I meant the Assembly Catechism by Watts).

"What is your name?"

"My name, sir?"

"Yes."

" -----"

"Who gave you that name?" I hesitated: - the question was repeated with an extra frown, and I replied,

"Uncle, sir; I think he wished me to be named aft - "

"Tut, tut; how have you brought up this boy, Mrs. B.?"

"If you please, sir," said mother in all proper humility, and with a profoundly reverent curtsey, "he goes to a Dissenting Sunday School."

"Yes, sir," I added, as bold as a quaker just seized on,

"I'm a Dissenter."

"Dear, dear, a youth like him talk in this manner! You ought to know better, B——. Can you read, boy?"

"Yes sir," (I could with truth have added - "a great deal better than you read the prayers to-day").

"Do you know the Lord's prayer?"

"Yes, sir."

"The Belief?"

"I believe not, sir."

"Well, you must learn all these things."

And so I did; and I don't know that I'm any the worse for it; perhaps better; but I do think that the *effects* of learning them would have been different, had the wandering sheep been kindlier treated by the shepherd. *He* didn't put me in his bosom, or even carry me on his shoulder to the fold, but he dragged me there, and that was *one* of the reasons at least, that I wandered again.

I was confirmed at Bow Church, (by the way, I have made a mistake - I have seen *two* Bishops; but upon my word, he who confirmed me, I don't know if he was fat or lean), - it was all a *task*.

After Confirmation, I sat on the same bench with mother, till one practice, which above all others, to my mind, young as it was, appeared even then absolutely revolting, caused me to leave: - the vile paupers partook of the Sacrament *after* the respectable among the congregation! Yes; when *they* had supped off the sacred elements, the lower orders had the leavings - Spiritual Lazaruses, waiting for the crumbs falling from a Saviour's table, the "Common-people's" Saviour.

A long way off, in the Southern States of America, black people take the Lord's Supper after the white people, and "talented lecturers," who can't bear black slavery (no more can I, or white slavery either) expatiate on this matter with "thrilling" eloquence, and amid loud cries of "shame, shame." Yet is this same damning insult to God and man perpetrated in our own Temples, and "talented lecturers" never think of crying "Woe, Woe." Never mind, my black and white brother slaves, The Eternal will set all to rights soon. The day is near, that great day - the books shall be opened, and the first shall be last, and the last first, Glory to God in the highest! This sure and certain hope, though, shouldn't deter us from speaking out on these matters. God hates wrong in all its forms, as much as we ought to hate it, and He will help them who help themselves.

The "Board" took 6d. a-week off the allowance three weeks after I refused to go any more to Church - I don't know *why*, because they wouldn't tell us, and I'm not going to *insinuate* any thing; but such was the fact; and if it was because of that refusal, why I won't grumble; to be fined only 6d. a-week for conscience sake is very cheap as the market goes. Ask France.

You must not suppose that I have not been to a Church since - I have many times - the first day, the service appeared very cold and dead-like, but that perhaps was, because I was so used to Dissenting forms of worship; for afterwards I gradually warmed towards it, and there is nothing in the Church service (which appears to me to be very Socialist), at all justifying such a scandalous separation of the Lord's people as I have just been describing.

Indeed, Dissenter as I am, (though for reasons Dissenters little think of,) I do love the idea of a National Church, but then it must be National; - a Church for the people - the poor man's Church, till there are no poor. Don't let's whitewash the thing.

"Well, what is to be done?"

Done! you have to *do* very little; your great work is to *undo* - fall back upon primitive principles and primitive practices; let there be *one* action, and there will soon be but one Lord, one Faith, and one Baptism. Hunt after the foxes less and the people more, and you will not have to hunt after them long; think of the "labour aggression," and you need not fear the "Papal aggression." Come to the help of the Lord against the mighty, and the mighty shall fall, and the weak your *real* strength, shall gather themselves together and take shelter under your protecting wing; they have gone under other wings and found them hollow; take advantage of this circumstance.

Many Dissenters have strayed farther from the good old way than you, and if they had the power would be much greater despots than you, with all your faults, have ever been.

Take advantage of this circumstance, I say, in your favour; and let the Spirit and the Bride say "Come," and we will come. Fewer creeds and more deeds and we *will* come.

This is my Slap at the Church, given, I appeal to God, in all humble sincerity. There must be something done by somebody soon.

Will you do it?

8

TRADE TRICKS AND SNOBBISM

My employer, the chemist, retired from business with, he admitted, a good round sum (the profits on physic are rather considerable), so I had to retire too, from that business, with half-a-crown he gave me - no doubt a fair share of the earnings we had accumulated during five years. Shortly after I got a place at Camberwell. The fact of its being so far from mother and school was unpleasant; but then, I had my victuals again - an important consideration - a good bed to lie on, for the first time in my life, and more enjoyed the pure air, to me, an unadulterated cockney, not so valuable but almost as yellow as a guinea, after seeing for so many years little else than mud; having an intimate acquaintance with tiles, but no knowledge of stiles; not remembering anything of fields, except of Spitalfields and Moorfields, which were no more fields than a horse-chestnut is like a chestnut horse. The change was like emigrating to another country - another world. I had lived previously for a long time in Whitecross Place, near Barbican.

It is said, God made everything. I don't believe it; He never made Whitecross Place, the entrance to which was the narrow way that leadeth unto stinks. A gutter passed through the middle of the court - a pretty looking gutter, from which the effluvia rose up, without ceasing, into our elegant second floor front; a room, or rather a cell (we paid 2s. 3d. rent weekly, for the blessed privilege of breathing in the accumulated filth below); a hole in which the bugs held a monster public meeting every night, determined to show what a co-operative movement could do.

I say, God never made Whitecross Place. He is not the author of filthy lanes and death-breeding alleys. Landlords and profit-mongers make them, and then proclaim national fasts to stay the progress of the cholera.

> "Be not deceived, God is not mocked;
> whatsoever a man soweth that shall he also reap."

Camberwell looked more like God's work, a great deal, and getting up as I did at daylight every morning, with my master, to help him to dig in his beautiful garden, made me so happy, and so healthy-looking during my five months' stay there, that my brother and sister Cockneyites scarcely knew me, when I returned to Dirtshire. I made a great mistake in leaving that place; not that the situation was over remunerative, or the master over kind. He kept a grocer's shop - that is to say he sold everything - a sort of co-operative store, of which he was the sole manager, and I the only member; doing all the cheating according to his order.

I will not be too hard upon him, though he *did* make the halfpenny bundles of wood smaller, by taking out the middle pieces for his own fire-side; though he *did* sell the same batter at three different prices, and performed other numerous innocent trade devices, by which he became a landlord, and builder of several houses, and was looked upon as a respectable man of some standing in society, too magnanimous to pick a pocket, and not hungry enough to steal a penny loaf.

I will not be too hard upon him, I say, for he salved his conscience every night by reading prayers, and every week by going to chapel. Beside, he was not worse than his glorious descendants, the chicory dealers in Fenchurch Street, and certainly not worse than the system that engenders and maintains so much hypocrisy and wrong, nor worse than my former employers to wit. The first would cut his ribbons and nearly everything else two yards shorter than their warranted value, and then sell them at an "enormous sacrifice;" for ever "selling off," yet never sold; a bottomless pit of "bankrupt's stocks." Every article he sold he lost at least fifty per cent by; yet did he live well by his losses, keeping his servants, and his country house at Norwood. How was it done? That question puzzled me for a long while, - how anybody could live by their losses - till one day an Irishwoman selling murphies explained it beautifully. Says she,

"Sir, by my *sowl* I loses by every tatie I sells."

"How do ye manage to live, then, Biddy?"

"Och, I sells so *many on 'em*, that's it."

Ay *that's* it, and the *many* fifty per cents W ----- lost kept his head above water. He'd have certainly sunk, had he lost *one* fifty per cent., but he took good care of that. Well, even my ham and beef man could oil his stale saveloys day after day, and ticket them as fresh Germans; so with my friend, the chemist, whose antibilious pills (I have made some thousands of them, God forgive me), were the best in all the world - proved so by hundreds of testimonials in the possession of the philanthropic inventor, whose self-interest was the last thing he dreamed of. The care of the afflicted was this philosopher's sole aim, and the only reason of his "twenty years' ceaseless study of that dire and excruciating pain, the head-ache." I don't think he lost much by his pills, or he'd have said so, for he was a man of strict truth, and benevolence, withal; advice was given gratis, which advice invariably ended in pills; gluttony in pills was a cardinal virtue - the more you took the better - for *him*. So with the Calvinist grocer, whose high, or rather low, antinomian principles had taken such deep root, that he thought no more of lying and cheating to save three farthings, than the Whigs do to save their places. And so used had I been for many years to help in these swindling transactions, that no qualms of conscience caused me to leave Camberwell but this:

On the 16th day of April, 1833, I was helping the servant to shake a carpet, in the lane, when her attention was directed to a woman who had fallen on the ground a little way off. I ran with her to assist, and it was mother - poor mother! She had gone to Greenwich College, that being her regular day to see her husband, and *did* see him, but it was in the "dead house," and then walked from there to Camberwell, to pour out her grief with the only soul she could, but the sight of me had unnerved her, and she fainted away on the high-road. It appears father had fallen suddenly ill, and though both our directions were with the nurse, she had omitted to let us know, hence our friend, without shaking hands with either of us, stepped into the river - *the river*.

His last words were, according to his attendant and fellow wardsmen,

> "Sweet fields beyond the swelling flood,
> Stand dressed in living green."

and so he swam over to the other side, without a murmur or a doubt.

"Ah," says some very clever reasoner, "his brain was turned;" yes, thank God, it was - the right way.

"May I die the death of the righteous, and my last end be like his."

> "A happy man, though on life's shoals,
> His bark was roughly driven;
> Yet still he braved the surge because
> His anchorage was in heaven."

We shall meet again. I would not lose that blessed faith for all the "*reasoners*" in the world. He was buried in the College ground, keeping death-company with those who had fought for their king, their country, and their grog. The warriors rest there in peace; when shall the hated name be altogether forgotten? Oh! for the hour when

> "*War shall die*, and man's progressive mind
> Soar as unfettered as our God designed?"

Oppression must cease first, though; let the Peace Society remember that.

Mother, who was never of a very strong mind, was this time nearly broken hearted, and she so earnestly begged of me to leave my place, and get one nearer *her*, that I did so, certainly against my own inclination, for the little surplus of money I had over and above my urgent necessities helped to comfort her. But I did leave it; and then began *again* a bitter struggle for bread. Week after week did I crave leave to toil; but, no; the curse which to me would have been a blessing, was denied, and destitution - the very poor know what I mean by that terrible word - was really felt by us. At last a cousin says to me:

"Why don't you learn the snobbing [unskilled shoe-making. Ed.], Jack; I'll teach you for nothing, and the first money that you earn you shall have."

"Agreed." (I dare say some of my readers think that my father might have learned me to shave; I think so, too; but, for some reasons or other, he ever had a repugnance to it, and that's all I can say in explanation.)

The first week of my "snobbing" we lived upon mother's pauper allowance, and the *last* two old chairs we sold for 1s. 9d. The second week I earned by "sewing" 1s. 10½d., and I lived on that with bread at 8d. a quartern loaf; a pound of which, and a "ha'porth" of treacle, was my day's allowance, with a halfpenny baked potato, and a suck at the pump, for my supper. Can any Vegetarian beat that? I had 4½d. left on Sunday, which I expended on threepen'orth of bread, a pen'orth of pea-soup, and my treacle. The next week I rose to 2s. 6d., and rose my extravagance in the same ratio, not saving a cent. The next week, 3s. 9d., a shilling of which I gave mother. *She* thought that I had had my victuals given me the last three weeks, but I deceived her, as she had often deceived me aforetime, by saying she had had a meal when she hadn't, in order that I might have it; so it was only tit for tat.

Well, after that "George" gave me 5s. a-week, for a month, and then I worked again for myself, and earned about 6s. weekly, not increasing for a long time, because each new part of the mystery shown me necessarily backened me for a while. At last, in less than a year, I became a snob, but not a *shoemaker*; not a tradesman. No; it would be harder for me to learn to make a *good* shoe, than perhaps, if I had never learned how to make a bad one. Cousin was what is called a "Chambermaster," - making up on his own account, "Bazil work;" and after buying leather, and all the etceteras, how much do you think he had for them? 1s. 4d., which was soon reduced to 1s. Mind, ladies, "spring heels," labour, materials, and all. Of course, the leather was of the worst description; the insoles only paper and oilcloth cuttings, from the dust yards, and the stitches - I can't *exactly* state their length, because we were never particular for an inch or so, but they were well black-balled over, to look tidy to the eye, and ticketed as ladies' shoes, of superior quality, only 1s. 9d. – the warehouseman and shopkeeper getting 9d. a pair between them, and the *maker* not above 3½d. Well may a friend of mine cry, "Cheap, cheap, cheap, means cheat, cheat, cheat."

Cousin managed, by the help of his wife cutting out and binding, and one of his children sewing, to earn a pound, or perhaps a little more, weekly, but I never could rise above 10s., and this by dint of hard and close work, so much so, that in two years I was nearly blind, and the doctor ordered me to abandon it at once, on pain of losing my sight altogether.

9

LOVE, MARRIAGE, AND BEGGARY

While I was a "Snob" I fell, (they may well call it *falling*), in love, and I proved myself quite as much a snob in *that*, as in trying to make shoes. There were some marvellously pretty girls, teachers in Artillery-street Sunday School, - most of whom got mated while there, as a reward, I suppose they thought, for their labours; but I loved the ugliest of the lot, as my wife will testify, who was *not* he ugliest of the lot, as she also is willing to testify. Mary B ---- with the small pox, bandy, and remarkably bad tempered. Yet, how I loved her, no "Lyrics of Love" can tell; and the many poems I wrote, and took them myself to her in order to save postage, and get *one* smile, which was hard enough to get, - I can tell you, by reason of her plurality of frowns, are too sublime for this periodical.

I *could*, I think, write a whole chapter on love-all about "divine images" and "angelic forms," - and how the sun shone when she smiled, and how all the stars looked dim when she didn't - for lovers can tell the weather by signs better than anybody else - but age, and reason, and the *one object* in writing this "auto," call on me to stay; nor should I have mentioned this circumstance at all, had not the fact of her jilting me three separate times (the false Bloomer!) been one of the principal causes of my leaving my first love - my Sunday School - and having led me thence by degrees to the very confines of atheism.

There were two young men in our school, called severally "David" and "Jonathan," from the fact of their being always together; and their hearts seemingly knitted together by long affection. We (for I was David) had joined the school together, got promoted together, distributed tracts together, joined the same church together, been baptised together, and - oh, tell it not in Gath! - kept company with the same woman together; but *that*, "David" didn't know, till one Sunday night, having missed her for a while, who should come into the Chapel but her own delicious self and - yes, and "Jonathan!" I was just going to give out a hymn, for which I immediately substituted another, commencing with

"How vain are all things here below,
How false, and yet how fair."

And I *did* sing it too, as spitefully as a disappointed one of five feet high well could. "Jonathan" carried off the prize. How she could have induced him - for it was she I'm sure - bothered me, but I attribute it to her tongue, which was of considerable length - most ladies' tongues are.

Well, nothing seemed to go right after Mary refused to be such a fool as to cast in her lot with a boy earning ten shillings a-week. The Chapel looked gloomy and desolate, and I quarrelled with everything. Even the parson I rebelled against - serve him right, though, for he was very proud and overbearing to us teachers, refusing even to let the scholars meet to sing; so I and one of the deacons headed a little band of malcontents, and opened an opposition shop to preach the gospel of brotherhood in; that deacon is now the minister of a flourishing congregation in the Tower Hamlets. After a time I left him too, and became Clerk at a little Chapel, the minister of which used nearly every Sunday to say that nobody but himself preached the truth; and so must his small congregation have thought, for when he died, they all split up into individuals, refusing to listen to any other man. What hard thoughts of God!

About this time I unfortunately got married, and I did very wrong. Without any clinging to the unnatural Malthusian doctrines, I own we did very wrong - both of us. Thank God I did not deceive her; she knew precisely my circumstances, and bitterly, very bitterly, have we suffered for our folly.

When I married, I was porter at twelve shillings a-week, at a place where they bound books for the Bible Society; - every man, woman, and child working there, distribute Bibles to the poor at a very cheap rate, with the words "British and Foreign Bible Society" outside; - and inside it is written "Cursed is he that grindeth the faces of the poor." Outside and inside - the comparison is indeed odious, - oh the cursings I have heard in that place! Not a soul throughout the establishment, that I knew of, even professed religious principles, except myself, and I got discharged for doing so. I was singing a hymn quite in a low tone while working; one of the mistresses happened to hear me and imperiously ordered me to desist, though songs were often sung among the binders up-stairs. I replied, that I thought it strange I couldn't praise God while working among Bibles, and so was immediately sent about my business. This was but three months after my marriage, and get another place I couldn't.

God knoweth I tried, as a drowning man would try to get to land, for our little home we had somehow scraped together - and which was much more comfortable than we have ever been able to get up since - was every week going – going - going, and our little child every week coming – coming - coming; and at last it came. That was a horrible day - the birth-day of my first boy! Wife, it was thought, would die; *and I knew why* die - from sheer staring want. No joy was in our nearly empty room, but all was desolate, and the very blackness of despair. "Why not apply to the parish?" Because ever since the day the guardian had told mother that he wouldn't "keep two of us," it ran in my head, and mother's too, that if I applied, her money would be stopped. It was a foolish idea, but we had nourished it for so many years that it became as it were a creed, and so rather than rob mother, as I thought, why, let us all die!

The next morning, that we might not die, I went to aunt's at Old Ford - my rich aunt's, she that had gotten her brother's money, - and she shut the door in my face. From thence I went to Brixton. "What for?" To sing, to beg, to cadge: I was thinking of omitting this portion of my life; but no, the truth shall be told - the whole truth.

That was a hard day's work, that 7th day of February, 1838. Fancy now; I, a hungry man, running before daylight (for I *did* run) all the way from Ray Street, Clerkenwell, to Old Ford, half hoping, half-despairing, half-mad, to a rich relation I despised, and whom I had not seen for years, to ask her for a miserable five shillings, because I knew her miserly, ugly heart - the being refused with the brutal taunt, that it "served me right and my fool of a wife too". The crawling back homewards down-spirited and ready to perish, with no text in all God's ward floating in my turning brain but job's wife's advice, "Curse God, and die," "Curse God, and die."

While wandering along Whitechapel Road, the sudden idea struck me that I would sing a hymn or two for bread and wife, and child - but I couldn't just there, known as I was all about the district. So on I went through the city, and passed over London Bridge, determined to begin at once, stepped into Thomas Street for that purpose, and then stepped out again; and thus I acted in several streets along the Borough. However, I *would* commence, *that* I would, when I got to the other side of the "Elephant and Castle." But no, courage failed again, and on I travelled. I will not weary my reader as I was wearied, by recounting my repeated trials, and my as repeated failures, till I got right on to Brixton. Necessity, it is said, has no law, and I began to feel the truism by then; nobody knew me there surely, and if they *did*, here goes - "God moves" - begin again - "God moves in a" - out with it, and so I did, almost choking,

"God moves in a mysterious way
His wonders to perform."

Just before I had concluded singing the hymn, a penny piece was thrown out, and without waiting to thank the donor, or even to give any further specimen of my vocal abilities, I pocketed the affront and went and spent it in Gin! "Oh you impostor!" - it is a lie! "Oh you drunkard!" - another lie! I was never drunk in my life, and I dare to say never an impostor. I own my first thoughts were for bread, but I felt too far gone for that, and an invisible spirit seemed to say, "Have some gin, it will give you courage." And so it did, whether false or true; it answered my purpose, for I went on again with energy to the tune of "Church Street," "God moves in a mysterious way," and then, hymn after hymn, and street after street, without flagging, while the coppers came rattling down like manna from heaven. Whether it was my singing loudly - for I had a good strong voice at that time, or my peculiar earnest manner, I know not, but, when I counted up my gains at about six o'clock, they amounted to six shillings, and, I think, fourpence. Heavy at heart, and yet much lighter than before, I laid out threepence in bread and cheese and beer, and began to march home, so tired, that in spite of my eagerness to see how things were, I did not reach it till late at night; and when I did, the first words that greeted me from her mother were,

"Hush, for God's sake, Jane is dying;" and from my mother,

"Why, John, my boy, you look dying too - where have you been to?"

"Oh I've been - don't bother me." And then a faint voice from the bed,

"John," - I ran to her side, and, says she,

"Where have you been to?" I whispered,

"I've got a place, my dear, got to go to-morrow, a good place, too - cheer up."

It was a lie! But a white one, and I believe it is not recorded against me in the book above. I then put the six shillings on the table, and sank into a chair exhausted.

"Why, where did you get all that money?" said both mothers at once,

"I've earned it," said I, "Well earned it - don't bother me."

And so I had earned it, for that was a hard day's work both for body and mind, was that same 7th day of February, 1838.

Quite as hard days, however, were yet in store - in the next chapter I will tell you all about it, and how and why I became a Rebel - a chapter I think of dedicating to my Lord John Russell, for he ought to know why men become Rebels.

10

HOW I BECAME A REBEL
DEDICATED TO MY LORD JOHN RUSSELL

The second morning of my begging experience, I took out sixpence, and afterwards was sorry for it, for somehow I *could not* begin my wretched toil, till all was expended, nor did I get rid of my last penny till towards evening.   During all these hours - for I started early - I must have travelled many miles, round the north of London, all the time, just *going* to begin, but not commencing.   When it was just dark, however, I summoned courage enough to strike up in a back street at Holloway,

> "O God, our help in ages past,
> Our hope for years to come."

No money: - then

> "Grace, 'tis a charming sound."

But no money.   Thinks I, I'll just sing my favourite "God moves," and then if nobody gives me anything, I'll just give up for to-day at any rate, - and nobody did, so home I went, and then saw doubly my folly, for Jane was still worse, and the money I had gotten the day before was nearly gone.   My mother's pauper allowance was all mortgaged for victuals eaten nearly a week ago, from a chandler's shop; and her mother was as poor as ourselves, not having had a place as monthly nurse - the labour on which she depended - for many months; and her husband, Jane's father - had left them and gone no one knew where, ever since his child was five years' old.

Well, on the third morning, after praying to God most heartily, that He would open a new path, and in the meantime, give me the courage of a Christian under these trying circumstances, (I note this fact, because I had not *really prayed* for some days, and because on that day I *did* seem to have more faith and courage), I went out, determined, as a punishment for my yesterday's weakness, to commence at once.   And sure enough, in Wilderness Row - a thronged thoroughfare, and not a quarter of a mile from my residence - begin I did, and got a halfpenny while singing a hymn.   Now, thought I, I've put my courage to the test, and paid penance into the bargain; but for fear I should be seen by those who know me, I'm off farther a-field.

At Islington I fairly began my day's work, and had scoured it well by two o'clock, with four shillings save one farthing, (a poor old woman *would make* me take a farthing, with many apologies that she hadn't more, God bless her), as my reward. I ran home with this sum, with the intention of going out again after an hour's rest. But fortitude failed when the stern necessity had temporarily hidden itself - *there was enough for the day*, and I didn't like my new business well enough to work at it till we were all getting hungry. Besides, I began already to think that, by perseverance, I could get any day enough food and something to spare, - in other words, could live much more comfortably by begging than by hard work.

Look at the *Tariff*, legislators, - 2s. for draining one's very life-blood out by incessant laborious toil, from six in the morning till eight at night - 3s. 11¾d. merely for asking *for* it, from nine till two P.M. Oh! if that idea had taken root, as it has taken root in thousands, spite of your treadmills and vagrant laws - what an accomplished beggar I'd have been by this time! This idea, however, was only a passing one with me, but mark - I got *bolder* every day.

The next day was Saturday, and I, by dint of keeping my sense of shame in the background for ten hours, managed to scrape up either a few halfpence under or over 7s. - I don't recollect which - but I do remember having a Sunday's hot dinner on the following day. No remarkable proof of my powers of memory by the way, for when a man has to go without a dinner for weeks and months consecutively, and then happens to make a mistake and get one, a hundred chances to one but he remembers the "why and because"; - dinner time comes regularly enough, but dinner and dinner time are not quite synonymous terms. I can't say that I much enjoyed my hot mutton and dumplings; for though wife had got somewhat better, she couldn't eat a bit, and the unceasing thinking of how I gained it, made me feel very uncomfortable; - not that I thought I had done wrong, nor do I think so now, but most certainly, a potato, with the knowledge that I had *sweated for it*, would have gone down much easier. On that day I sang too, but then it was in the dark at S—es Street Chapel, Bethnal Green. The congregation little thought when I gave out, with a deep sigh,

"God moves in a mysterious way,"

that I had sung it scores of times on the previous days in the streets! Ah! the heart only knoweth "its own bitterness," a wise arrangement.

On Monday morning (pardon, reader, if I weary you by being so particular, - I am telling, as briefly as I can, of eight days of real agony, and the telling of it seems to relieve me even at this hour) - on Monday morning, after, - like a "giant refreshed" with two strong cups of tea and a bit of yesterday's mutton, I started off for Brixton again, with this idea, that I'd go day after day the same round, once more, saving every farthing over necessities, for capital to buy things to sell again in the streets, - *that* was better than begging. Well, I got but 2s. 9d. all day - yes, I got something else - a threat to be sent to the "Mill" just handy. [Millbank Prison. Ed.]

"That'll cure you of your singing about here, I'll *warrant*,"

said a gentleman to me - what a many spurious things people do *warrant* to be sure! Now that gentleman was no social doctor at all, though he might have been one of the many social *quacks*. Being sent to the "Mill" would not have cured me, or at least if it had cured me of *that* disease, it would have perhaps brought on a worse - thieving. Prisons are not *hospitals* for social disorders, I'll *warrant*, though they ought to be, I'll warrant.

Tuesday, had 1s. 7d. I was out many hours too, but very low-spirited. Just as I was going to commence, I met a person I had known from childhood - an old schoolfellow; we talked over the days that were gone, and when we parted, the reminiscence seemed like a cold weighty stone at my heart. He went on his way, not knowing of my day's task; - if he had, he would have helped me, I believe, with his last penny; - but then he was poor, and nothing seemed so recoiling to me as that any one should know what I did for my bread.

I think it was on this day that I began singing in a street where some other beggar, with a woman and two children was imploring the inhabitants for relief. I didn't notice him at first, but he soon called me aside, and with a terrible oath said he'd kill me if I dared to oppose him. I tried to explain, but to little purpose, and we parted with the comfortable assurance from him

"That I was either *jolly green* or a b----y rogue, and that if I didn't know that to come and cadge in a street where another cadger was *working*, was not against the *rule* in the "Siety," he'd make me know it by jumping my guts out."

I think I hear the ejaculation, "*There* was a wretch past all redemption." Nonsense; he might have been redeemed with very little trouble; there was at least the germ of something good in that man; ay, that *man* - his sentiment was manly after all; if you take away the chaff, and the rough way in which it was delivered, and *sift* it well, the wheat will appear, meaning simply this, "Don't enter into such public competition with your fellow-man, and thus rob him of his share - there's room enough for all, if you'll only give *all* fair play."
The man was right, and so was the "Siety."

Wednesday. A very lucky day; 9s. and odd - including a half-crown a lady gave me.

"Ma'am, this is a half-crown."

"I'm aware of that," says she, as a tear started to her beautiful eye. "God bless you!"

"And God bless you," I repeated, "Pray let me tell you *why* I am thus;" –

but no, with another most benevolent look, she vanished. I have often thought she knew me; whether or not, she did right, and she did wrong. She *happened* to do right by giving that half-crown to *me*, because I expended it properly, but she did wrong in not inquiring and ascertaining first. The people who give half-crowns away in the streets must have good hearts, but not very sound judgements; they err on the right side, but still they err. If benevolent people would give with judgement, not depending on any society, but on their own *personal observations*, they would do twenty times more good, and save half their money. In all my eight days' cadging experience, I was never asked a question; so I might have been an impostor all the while. Well, well, better give an impostor now and then money, by mistake, than miss the blessed opportunity of saving a poor starving wretch from dying, by withholding a penny, or even half-a-crown, if God has made you steward of a good many.

I put away, out of the 9s., 5s., with the determination to begin on Saturday with that trifle, if I couldn't get more, by the sale of memorandum books, and other stationery. On Thursday morning, going along Fleet Street, or the Strand, I saw, what I looked out for every day in my travels - a bill up in a window, for "A Man Wanted;" and I lost three parts of the day before I could get an answer. And the anxiety I felt - the war between hope and fear, all those hours - was very severe. "Call again in an hour;" then "another hour," and so on. At last the lottery turned up a blank. He couldn't take me, because I'd been out of work so long, "Six months, and above; oh, dear no." Suppose I'd told him what I had been doing the previous week, it *would* have been an "O, dear, no," most heartily given. *That's it*, you see. Once an outcast, mind what you're at; if you are only hungry six hours, why they'll give you to eat, but if hungry six months, O, starve away, or beg, or steal, there's plenty of workhouses and jails for such obstinate burdens, and we pay rates, and very heavily too, to keep them out of our sight. God save the Queen! I went on late that afternoon to Chelsea, sick at heart with hope delayed, and then - as it had been many times before - blasted - and took seventeen pence, the last money I got by singing in the streets.

The next day I became a Rebel, and this was how it was, "Lord John," - all facts, without a comment. Going up Holborn on Friday morning, I met a man carrying a board with bills on it, having words to the following effect: -

Give no money to beggars, - food, work, and clothing, are given away to them by applying to the Mendicity Society, Red Lion Square.

What, food, work, clothing, given away! O! here's good news! Let them give me work though, and I'll find food and clothing myself.

"I say, governor," to the man with the board, "what's all that mean?"

"What's all what mean?" said as comical a looking figure-head as any Great Exhibition directed by phrenologists could well produce.

"That bill."

"Vy, dos'ent yer know?"

"No."

"Vell you is raw, and no flies."

Now what this distinguished agent of the Association meant by *raw*, I did not then comprehend, and what flies had to do with his reply is also a mystery which future enlightened generations must unravel; for he didn't tell, and I didn't ask him. I wanted just then to get at something else.

"Do, my good fellow," said I, "pray do tell me if I really *can* get food, work, and clothing, and how."

"Is yer a beggar?"

"No - yes."

"Now none of yer lies, 'cos if yer isn't a beggar, the gemmen vont giv yer not nuffin."

"I am, I am, my friend."

"Vell then, you must get a ticket."

"A ticket?"

"Yes, or it's not no account I tells yer."

"And how am I to get a ticket?"

"Vy go to Russell Square, or any o' them air grand cribs, and axxe the first gemman you meets."

"Shall I say you sent me?"

"O no, yer fool; jist axxe, I tells yer, for a ticket for the Mendickety Siety, and they'll give it yer, and then take it to the place what's directed, and then (with a leer - such a leer!) you'll see what you will see."

I thanked him, and started for Russell Square, full of wonderment. Sure enough, I *did* get a ticket, of the third person I asked. Here was fortune! - food, work, clothing, by just applying for it; and I had not known of it before; well, I was a fool, as the man just told me. Food, work, clothing! and with joy and boldness I knocked at the office door in Red Lion Square.

"What do you want," said the opener.

"Here's a ticket, sir," (showing it for fear he wouldn't believe me) "I want to see the gentlemen inside."

"O, go round the corner; that's *your* way," and he slammed the door in my face.

Ah! stop till I see the gentlemen, *they'll* not speak to me so, thought I, as I went round the corner, and down some dirty steps. And then such a scene presented itself to me as never can be effaced from my memory! A hundred - fully a hundred, of the most emaciated, desolate, yet hardened, brutal - looking creatures, were congregated together in the kitchen, the majority of them munching, like so many dogs, hunks of bread and cheese. I was told to pass on, and then another hundred daguerreotype likenesses of the first hundred met my bewildered gaze, waiting to pass a wooden bar one by one. Of course I had to stay my turn; and not knowing how to be "jolly" with them - for even these neglected miserable wretches were jolly - I got finely chaffed. I dare not attempt to write their filthy remarks; - one man, however, in all that Devil's crowd, took pity on the "green one," and I began to tell him all about the food-work-and-clothing idea, which still kept wandering about my brain, though it seemed trying to find an outlet as if tired of stopping there. I shall never forget how heartily he laughed, as I related to him my affair with the board-man, - Bill Somebody, of the "Dials," whom he appeared to know very well. After informing him how long I had begged, and pretty well all my circumstances, he said to me,

"I tells you what, old flick, you've been deceived, its all lies. They only give you a bit of bread and cheese, and you must be up to snuff to get *that*, - not one in a hundred gets more. Clothing's all my eye. And them as gets work, it's to break stones at six bob a-week. Its all lies I tell you."

Now by this time I scarcely knew who to believe - the gentlemen who advertised such good things, or the poor beggar who had branded them as liars. But in about an hour longer, I found out. It was my turn to pass the barrier - I was ushered into a room by a beadle, and stood behind another bar like a criminal; and on the other side sat six gentlemen, as people call bears that are dressed well; when the following dialogue, nearly word for word, took place, between me and the chairman:

"Well, what do you want?"

I fumbled for my prize ticket, and said,

"Here's a ticket, sir, - a gentleman gave me in Russell Square."

"Well, well, what do you want, I say?"

"If you please sir, I met this morning a man carrying a board on which was stated that I could get food, work, and clothing, - but I only want work, sir."

"Are you a beggar?"

"Yes, sir."

"How long?"

"Eight days."

"Only eight days, - are you sure of that?" (with a cunning infidel leer).

"Yes, sir, that is all."

"Are you married?"

"Yes, sir."

"Ah, I thought so. How many children have you got?"

"One, sir."

"O, I wonder you didn't say a dozen - most beggars say a dozen. How do you beg?"

"I sing hymns, sir."

"O, one of the pious chanters," - with a grin at the gentlemen, who grinn'd too, at his brilliant wit.

"Have you applied to your parish?"

"No, sir." *That* did it, - that *truth*, - if I had told a lie, the wrath of his worship the Chairman might in time have been assuaged, but telling the truth proved I was not "*up to snuff*," for in a loud, angry voice he called the officer, and thus addressed him, -

"Officer, you see that fellow - you'll know him again - he goes about singing hymns; he says only eight days, - is that a truth?"

"O dear no," said the lying scamp, "I've known him for years!"

"Ah, now, mark him well, watch for him, and directly you catch him, lock him up, and send for me. We'll have this gentleman before a magistrate, and he shall sing hymns on the treadmill."

Now its some time before I break loose, but when I do, I never stay at a half-way-house - all the way there and no stoppages, - is my motto; so I retaliated, as every honest man ought to do when he's insulted and belied by a thing that feeds on him according to law. I retaliated, I say, with equal warmth, calling him a liar (a scriptural phrase by-the-bye) point-blank, and all the *gentlemen* too; -

"You advertise lies", said I, "wholesale, now lock me up, and I'll show the magistrate and the world that you are the impostors, and obtain money under false pretences from the benevolent."

Well to be sure, I expected to be collared every moment. Yet I fired away, bang, bang, till I was more than a match for the Chairman, who at last listened staring, without saying a word, but just a grunt now and then, like a pig as he was. One of the *gentlemen* at length said,

"Give him some bread and cheese, and let him go,"
(I was hungry enough, for not a bit of anything had I tasted since eight in the morning, and then it was late in the afternoon).
　　Well, they gave me another *prize* (!) ticket, entitling me to half-a-pound of bread and a piece of cheese, and I went back into the kitchen to get it, pocketed it, and was about to sheer off, when the beadle stopped me and ordered me to eat it there.

"I shall not," said I.

"You must."

"I won't."

"Then give it back."

"I won't do that either."

"Then come along with me," and I was again before the immortal six.

"Sir, he won't eat his bread and cheese."

"O, then let him give it back."

"He won't do that, sir."

"You must, sir," said the Chairman to me.

"I won't."

"You must, I tell you, it's the rule, and you must obey it."

"I don't care about your *rules*, I want to share it with those I love, who are as hungry as I am, and if you are a Devil with no natural feelings, I am not. Get out of the way, beadle," and out I rushed, like one mad, through the crowd of astonished beggars, right into the street, without one stopping me.

After I had got home, and told them of my adventures, (I had told them of my *singing propensities* a day or two before), I went downstairs to the landlord to pay him a week's rent out of the four I owed him, and the good fellow said,

"Never mind, if you haven't yet got any work, I don't take any till you do, I'm sure you'll pay me - how long have you been out of work?"

"Near seven months," I said, with a sigh, thinking more of the dogs I had encountered in the day than anything else.

"Ah," says he, "there'll be no good done in this country till the *Charter* becomes the law of the land."

"The Charter?"

"Yes, I'm a Chartist - they meet to-night at Lunt's Coffee House on the Green - will you come?"

"Yes."

It was only a "Locality" meeting, but there were about sixty people present, and as one after another got up, oh, how I sucked in all they said!

"Why should one man be a slave to another? Why should the many starve, while the few roll in luxuries? Who'll join us, and be free?"

"I will," cried I, jumping up in the midst. "I will, and be the most zealous among you - give me a card and let me enrol."

And so, Lord John, I became a Rebel; that is to say: - Hungry in a land of plenty, I began seriously for the first time in my life to enquire WHY, WHY - a dangerous question, Lord John, isn't it, for a poor man to ask? lending to anarchy and confusion

Well, but it wasn't my fault, you know. When *you* are out of *a place*, you are about the first one to cry there's something wrong. Now I was out of *a place*, and so I cried the same. Politics, my Lord, was with me just then, a bread-and-cheese-question. Let me not, however, be mistaken; I ever loved the idea of freedom, - glorious freedom, and its inevitable consequences, - and not only for what it will fetch, but the *holy principle*; - a democrat in my Sunday School, everywhere - and whether the sun shines on my future pathway, or the clouds look black as they have ever done, neither sun nor cloud shall alter my fixed principle.

> "A boy I dreamt of liberty;
> A youth - I said, but I am free;
> A man - I felt that slavery
> Had bound me in her chain.
> But yet the dream, which, when a boy,
> Was wont my musings to employ,
> Fast rolling years shall not destroy,
> With all their grief and pain."

[The end of Bezer's 'Autobiography.']

Part of the Strand c. 1825. Showing the site of the modern Burleigh House and Strand Palace Hotel

5.

CIRCULATION OF THE *CHRISTIAN SOCIALIST*

The following letter, written by Bezer - as Publisher of the *Christian Socialist* - was inserted in the issue of 5 December 1851 in response to an appeal for more readers, but the *Christian Socialist* was discontinued from issue No. 61, 27 December, 1851.

CIRCULATION OF THE *CHRISTIAN SOCIALIST*.
THE CHARTIST REBEL TURNED SPY—
BUT NOT IN THE PAY OF THE GOVERNMENT.

A "free" letter, partly auto-biographical, but very much out of order.

Dear Sir,

When I read your "Appeal" in No. 53, [1November1851] of this Journal, the first words I uttered were the chorus of one of the songs of Mackay, I think –

"There *must* be something wrong;"

and being convinced of the soundness of those first words with reference to that "appeal," I went on a voyage of discovery, to find out what that something was; or, in other words, I enrolled myself as a member of the "Detectives" not so much to spy out the nakedness of the land as the cause of it.

As I took notes on my way, more especially as I travelled "Through Finsbury Fields, on ye road to Bethnal," will you permit the insertion of them in your "Free Correspondence." What I said, and what I heard - how, in going down to Jericho, I fell among thieves, and all about it.

The first thing I did was to have an interview with the publisher - an intimate friend of mine, Sir, as you are aware, and who I knew would tell me everything "without reserve," as the linen-drapers say when they want to get rid of a slop article.

"How is it, my dear B.," said I, "that the circulation of the *Christian Socialist* is so miserably low, though the recognised organ of a practical movement, numbering its thousands of members, 'cute far-seeing souls, determined to do what Sir Robert Peel told them to do, take their affairs into their own hands?"

"Why" says he, "there are several reasons, but two only I'll tell you just now, and the rest another time. One is, that some of the chaps are *too 'cute*, for while saving *pounds* annually through joining the co-operative cause, they are afraid of *spending* a penny to keep it up. And the second is, that some are not *'cute enough*, not having heard as yet even of the existence of the periodical, as letters on my file will show."

"Why, how is that?" cried I, struck all of a heap.

"Ah, that's it - it hasn't been properly pushed;" and then, whispering in my ear, "it hasn't been *puffed*."

"Puffed!" I exclaimed with horror; "how can you mention so detestable a word with reference to such an anti-puffing journal as this?"

Well, at that I *did* catch it, for what he chose to call my short-sightedness, telling me that –

"Puffing according to truth, was a very different thing to puffing according to lies. That if a man sold coffee without mixing it with chicory, he had a right to say so. That those who love truth *ought* - it was their holy duty - to compete with those who love falsehood - by proclaiming it on the house-tops, and zealously asking everybody they can get at, Who is on the Lord's side? That in this enlightened age; this middle of the 19th century, the "glorious many," the "sovereign people," thought truth so valuable, that you must just take it to them without any trouble on their parts, for the deuce a bit would they come and fetch it, or even enquire after it, till they had once tasted it. Then, *ah then*, eating will increase their appetite, and they'll cry, give, give, as if in a galloping consumption. That therefore, "as the supper was quite ready, one must go into the highways and hedges, and compel them to come in," and so he went on jabbering away,

"How that he'd told a few gentlemen his views, and they, being as sensible as himself, (as he is rather conceited), they had cheerfully subscribed £14 for that purpose; how that he had spent £17 *out of it*, (he would make a good Chancellor of the Exchequer, I must admit, if that be a fact), in large showbills, and handsome window-cards, and inserting advertisements in several newspapers, and sending a "Perambulator" round the metropolis, announcing that a portrait of "Parson Lot," (who is a very good lot, by the way), would be given with No. 56.

How that in consequence of the sale of No. 55, had nearly doubled; that the back numbers were being sent for, wholesale, retail, and for exportation, by parties who had never heard of it before, or who had been told that it was dead; how that 500 extra copies had been printed of No. 56, because he fully expected that people would, that week at any rate, run for *Christian Socialists*, as in times of panics they run for gold; how that,"—

"Now, stop, stop," said I, "and do rest that tarnation tongue of your's. I had a long tongue once and got into Newgate through it: mum, the proof of the pudding's in the eating. Just give me a few quires of the portrait-number, and some bills and cards, and I'll go round 'the trade' with 'em."

And so I began my tour eastward.

It has been said, Sir, that that lawyers (beg your pardon, Sir), and printers, and newsvendors, are an unholy, inglorious trinity, having no consciences, and willing to do anything to earn a crust. I am not versed enough in the law to speak *positively* of the first class, and I shouldn't like being indicted for a libel. Of the second class, I am *afraid* to speak, inasmuch as the Co-operative Printers are all bigger men than myself. But a number of the third class, I hesitate not to declare, have been most maliciously belied - to wit: - In one shop I went into, the man said, in reply to my request that he would put a bill up, after looking at it as if it were a *Red Republican*, with a pike in his hand,

"No Sir, couldn't do it, conscience wouldn't allow me."

"Conscience!" I ejaculated in surprise, not having heard the word before in a newsvendor's shop.

"Yes, Sir, *conscience* - Socialist! Socialist! O dear no."

"Well, but *Christian Socialist*."

"Ah, it's all one, all one - it's a revolutionary thing, I know it is, and wants to upset the government. But I'm a respectable man," puffing himself out like a bloater full roed, and doubtless thinking at the moment of the 10th of April, and that dear, dear, special constable's staff in the parlour.

"*I'm* a respectable man, and won't sell it - and that's flat."

Readers of Mister Lloyd's elevatting, moralizing, instructive murder-tales, go feast your eyes on the large blood-red pictures, those splendid triumphs of art, portraying as they do, so accurately, how easily one man can cut another man's throat, and then go inside, and ask for a penn'orth of mental laudanum, and you'll not be disappointed; but Christian Socialists, go not near the shop, for the *respectable* proprietor thereof has a conscience, and a remarkable one.

There were many as bad as he, and some still worse, for they would promise to expose the bills, and then shove them into the waste place; (these were the thieves I spoke of just now, while going down to Jericho) - so feeling that hypocrites had no time redeeming quality, I went back for them; *Christian Socialist* bills shall not be torn up at three half-pence per pound, if I know it. However, I sold the lot I took out, and a goodly number of shops have them exposed, a list of which I'll give next week. [List not published. Ed.] I mention this, because the publisher tells me, that a great many readers of this journal go to *him* and buy, a very bad arrangement. They should go anywhere but to him. If every reader will buy at the nearest shop that agrees to put a bill up, it will be so many standing advertisements gratis. Let every reader take this hint, and the sale must steadily increase, without a farthing extra outlay.

Well, as I crossed Finsbury Square, I met the man with the perambulator, and a rare crowd was round him, I tell you, asking each other what on earth Christian Socialism meant? A very nice-looking gentleman, however, in a blue coat, and pretty looking figures on it, *blandly expostulated* with the breaker of the law, telling him as mildly as the breed can, "that he'd take it to the green-yard, if he didn't move on." [The Green Yard was on the east of Whitecross Street, where stray horses, cattle and carriages were impounded. Ed.] But brother M. wasn't *green* enough to let him, for he *did* move on, but so slow, that one would have thought it were a hearse at a funeral, while the wondering spectators, like so many mourners, kept following, and reading on.

Just as I was selling off the last remnant of my stock, in Brick Lane, a large bill attracted my attention, the subject of which, though not directly concerning this Journal, has certainly some reference to its objects. It said,

Old Church, Bethnal Green.
Persons can get married, banns, certificates, &c., included, for 5s.

Halloa, thought I, Solomon, who for a *king* was not a fool, said that a virtuous woman was *worth a crown* to her husband; but I knew not till now you could buy her at the price, when lo! close by the former bill, was stuck up another to the following effect –

> Marriages solemnized at the *New* Church, Bethnal Green; banns, and certificate included, only 2s. 6d.

Hurrah! Here was competition in the churches! Therefore, let the rallying cry of Free-traders be - not a Free-trade and a cheap loaf, but - "Free-trade and a cheap wife." The Chartist Rebel's advice to persons about to be married - *Don't*! or if you do, don't fool your money away, but go to the cheap slop churches, the spiritual Moses [Note: the Editor of the *Christian Socialist* inserted a comment at this point - "Wrong, friend Rebel - it does not follow that a cheap church is a slop church, nor are low marriage-fees the result of sweating and grinding."] and Sons, who, at enormous sacrifice, are nearly giving away wives and husbands, to the great joy of Cupid and the holy horror of the ghost of Malthus.

As I returned home, I ruminated, not so much on political as *domestic* economy: here had I been married fourteen years, and the balance sheet ran thus - *Lost*, 10s.; *gained*, 9 children. Oh! if I had but waited for the good time at last to come! Well, if I ever do meet the parson of Christchurch, Newgate Street, who charged me the immense sum of 12s. 6d. for a little woman not five feet high, when I could have one nearly twice her size for 2s. 6d., I'll just ask for my money back. And so, in high dudgeon, I went back to Fleet Street, and thus ended my first day's tour. My second, third and fourth were much about the same, and the repeating them would be tautology. Suffice it, that by the time this letter appears, not a number of 56 will be in print, except in the Thirteenth Part, ready last Saturday, and with which a portrait of Mr. Kingsley is given.

And so the publisher and I - and indeed several others - feel that the journal has not as yet had *fair play*; and that if the same energy is kept up for the next three months as has been shown the last fortnight, the sale will increase to 5,000 weekly in that time, without reducing the size or raising the price (pray don't do either, Mr. Editor, or you'll commit suicide.) Of course, this wants money. The wall must come down without battering-rams. It has therefore been proposed that a "Three Months' *Christian Socialist* Advertising Fund" shall be opened, to which the following have already subscribed: -

	£.	s.	d.
Thomas Hughes, Esq	1	0	0
Rev. Charles Kingsley	1	0	0
Professor Maurice	5	0	0
A Lady Friend	1	0	0
W. Lees, Esq	1	0	0
F.T.V.		5	0
Vansittart Neale, Esq	5	0	0
A Chartist Rebel		5	0

I am, Sir, yours very truly,
THE CHARTIST REBEL.

FROM *THE ILLUSTRATED LONDON NEWS*
Feb. 23, 1850.

STATE OF NEWGATE.

THE Rev. J. Davis, the Ordinary of Newgate, has just presented to the City authorities the report of the State of the Prison from Sept. 30, 1848, to Sept. 29, 1849. From this interesting document we learn that, during the above period, there were in the Gaol –

Unconvicted Prisoners	588
Convicted	1111
Convicted of very grave offences	938
Making a total of	2637
Of which number there have been	
Previously in Newgate	345
in other Prisons	385
	730

The returns for the previous year, to Sept. 29, 1848, were:-

Unconvicted Prisoners	645
Convicted	1418
Very grave offences	1070
Decrease under	
Unconvicted	57
Convicted	307
Very grave offences	132
	496

Making a general diminution of nearly 500, or nearly one-sixth of the whole number committed.

The reverend Ordinary observes:

> The gaol of Newgate, beyond all doubt, has great defects compared with more modern erections; but results from these more perfect prisons do not surpass the metropolitan gaol in this respect, that seven out of eight do not return to us again.
> Another gratifying point is the great decrease in the number of boys committed, and great change in committers.

It is greatly to be desired (continues the Report) that no sentences (except for very short periods) should take place in Newgate. The perpetual excitement, the over fluctuating character of the inmates, the assemblage of criminals of the most flagrant nature, the constant recurrence of the sessions, make Newgate a very undesirable prison for purposes of lengthened confinement.

The great corruption of Newgate still appears to be most fearful in the transport wards. The condition of the transports, confined for months in perfect idleness, makes them spend their leisure time in awfully corrupting one another. The language, acts, and habits of these utterly depraved men; their filthiness, falsehood, and pernicious animosities; are too bad to be described. The magistrates wish these men removed to their proper place of confinement. The Government are unable to comply with these reasonable desires, because every place is full. The rev. Ordinary than suggests the fitting up of wards as workshops, as in Millbank prison, and the keeping of the offenders constantly at labour; and this matter is pressed the more earnestly, because it has been the cause of all the calumnies that have found their way into many public documents as to the corruption inside of Newgate.

There is another part of the prison that demands attention - the separate cells, which the Report states are so intensely cold in inclement weather, that the pain which the prisoners suffer is almost to the full extent of human endurance.

We annex a series of views of the interior of this metropolitan prison. Up the narrow steps, into the turnkey's room, and along a darkish passage, we come into a small open court, surrounded by high walls, between which a scanty supply of air and light finds its way downwards as into a well. Facing us stands a massive building, chary of windows, and those strongly grated: it is the women's wing of the prison. As soon as the ponderous locks are turned, and the heavy bar removed, we enter the doorway, and ascend the stone staircase: suites of chambers branch off on either side, and these are occupied by the prisoners who are awaiting trial. An attempt is made to classify them according to their degrees of godliness, but practically this is of little use.

Pass we now through several rooms and corridors through the quadrangle occupied by the males. As we traverse these passages we note the iron character of the building. It is dark, close, confined; and in despite of the scrupulous cleanliness preserved in every part, foul smells are not unfrequently met in its lobbies. The great fault is the want of room, the height of the walls, and the narrowness of the courts, giving them the appearance of wells rather than open spaces. Air and light are in consequence less plentiful than they should be.

Formerly the wards of part of this prison were occupied by debtors. This practice has been discontinued, and it has now very few inmates, except such as are awaiting trial or punishment; the exceptions being persons convicted of assaults or offences on the high seas. Just after the termination of the session of the Central Criminal Court it is nearly empty, but it gradually begins to fill again as the next assize draws nigh; then its inmates usually number about 500. After trial the convicts are sent off to prisons or penitentiaries to which they are committed - the short terms to the Houses of Correction, the transports to Millbank. Those sentenced capitally are taken to the condemned cells, not to leave them again until the last moment, except for chapel. These cells are built in the old portion of the building at the back. The narrow port-holes in the dark wall looking into Newgate-street let light into the galleries into which they open. There are five of them on each of the three floors. The culprit in the furthest cell on the ground-floor is within a yard of the passers-by. All the cells are vaulted, and about nine feet high, nine deep, and six broad. High up in each is a small window, double-grated. The doors are four inches thick. The strong stone wall is lined; and, altogether, they present to the eye of the culprit an overwhelming appearance of strength. In a small ante-room, near the entrance of the prison, is a collection of casts, taken from the heads of the principal malefactors who have been recently executed in front of it - very interesting to the student of phrenological science.

The quadrangle for the men is much like the women's, but larger. It consists of two or three yards, and the building surrounding them. No separation of the men is made other than as the law requires - namely, into felons and misdemeanants.of the same height as the lofty houses in Newgate-street, and present a bar to Some little instruction is afforded by humane and philanthropic visitors at the prison, especially of ladies. Dear Elizabeth Fry used to make the female wards the scene of her pious labours. She found helpers and successors in the work. Lady Pirie is a constant visitor and teacher here now - so is Miss Sturgiss. They read, converse, and pray with their poor sisters.

The chapel, as well befits such a place, is neat and plain. There are galleries for male and female prisoners. Below and in the centre of the floor, a chair is placed conspicuously, and marked for the use of the condemned culprit. On this he is required to sit the day before his execution in face of the congregation.

Leaving the chapel we repass the yards, one of which is notable as the scene of a very curious escape - that of the "sweep." The walls are escape which would daunt the most inveterate prison-breaker. But the sweep surmounted them. Placing his back in the angle of the wall, he worked himself up by his hands and feet, pressing them against the rough masonry, until he reached the giddy height. He then crept along the top or the walls to the houses, got on to the roofs, entered at a balcony - almost frightening a woman to death - and made his way into the streets, where, as the Newgate prisoners wear no regular costume, he passed unnoticed. He was, however, captured soon after - as almost invariably happens with escaped criminals. Now the wall is smoothed and spiked, there can be no escapes in that way.

We have selected these descriptive details from Mr. Dixon's recently published work on the Great Prisons of London.

PART TWO

AUSTRALIAN FINALE

Until now it has been assumed that John James Bezer had emigrated to Australia in 1852, there to remain an anonymous figure. But an 1861 census return for Bethnal Green gives his name as head of the family, and the marriage certificate of his last daughter in 1868 states that he was deceased (see Part One).

However, a communication including documents, articles, and photos received from Norman W. Drew, Bezer's Great Grandson in Australia, confirms otherwise.

I am therefore grateful to Norman Drew who has kindly permitted me to use the information that he supplied, together with the photographs.

It appears that Bezer went to Australia after July 1852 (either as an emigrant or by paid passage), though he has not been traced through passenger lists, which are incomplete.

The first record of Bezer in Australia is of a marriage between him and Elizabeth Roberts, aged 25, on the 11 May, 1854, at Christ Church, Geelong, Victoria. Geelong, where Bezer was residing at that time, is some 40 miles south-west of Melbourne. His wife's residence was in Chilwell, a suburb west of Geelong, now encompassed by Newtown

In the marriage certificate he gave his name as John Bezer Drew (his mother's maiden name), born in London. He stated also that he was a widower, his wife, whose maiden name (in a later certificate) he gave as Jane Bridge, having died on 28 May 1851. He had one child living, and three deceased, and gave his occupation as a shoemaker. His father's name he stated as James Drew, hairdresser, and his mother's maiden name as Mary Stevens.

His new wife, originally Elizabeth Burl, came from Lambeth, London. She had married Frederick Roberts who died in Australia on the 18 July 1853 after only 9 months marriage. There was one child by the marriage, but this has not been traced.

John Drew (John Bezer Drew's second son) with his wife Elizabeth on their
wedding day 1891

Their first son, Thomas Bezer Drew, was born on the 12 February 1855 at Creswick. John Bezer Drew's occupation given as a shoemaker. Creswick is 75 miles north west of Melbourne, and was commencing then as a gold mining town. It had a growing population of some 25,000.

Their second child, Elizabeth Charlotte Drew was also born at Creswick, on the 10 August 1856, her father listed now as a newsagent. Between then and 1858 the family moved 60 miles on to Ararat, another gold mining town, newly established, with a population of some 9,000 within the area.

The map illustrated shows the towns where the family stayed in relation to Melbourne, to which the family finally moved:

Melbourne and area

Two years following, in 1858, their third child, John Drew, was born also at Ararat on the 25 March (John Bezer Drew a Fruit Vendor), with their fourth, Mary Burl Drew the following year, on the 22 December 1859. John Bezer Drew now stated to be a Storekeeper.

During John Bezer Drew's time in Australia, he proved himself as versatile – and indeed as volatile – as in his previous years in London. Although he was never engaged in goldmining, he took advantage of the variety of new jobs opening up and found employment variously as a Newsagent, Commission Agent, Fruit Vendor, Letter Deliverer and Newspaper Correspondent, among others. In 1861 in Ararat, Mary Burl Drew died from whooping cough on the 1 February aged 13 months. John Bezer Drew stated to be a Shoemaker at that time. It was noted later that he had been a prolific and witty correspondent for the local *Ararat*

Advertiser in the early 1860's. He is mentioned also in Christine Gibbs' *History of Postal Services in Victoria* (1984), that John Drew, an enterprising man, was a Town Crier in Ararat, where he organised a Post Office Association. Members of the Association could have their letters delivered by Mrs Drew and the family for a shilling per week.

Later that year the family moved some 20 miles from Ararat to Pleasant Creek (Stawell), where Amelia Bezer Caroline Drew was born on the 21 September. Whilst at Pleasant Creek he was the representative of the *Ararat Advertiser*, as well as again diversifying his talents by offering to write letters for residents, in confidence. One commentator referred to him as being 'a very small stout man.' Politically he remained an ultra-democrat by supporting John Woods (1822-1892) an engineer, originally from Liverpool, and a member of the Legislative Assembly (*The Golden Years of Stawell*, 1983). Woods had supported the Anti-corn law League when in England, and in Australia remained committed to democratic and radical principles.

The picture illustrated shows Upper Main Street, Pleasant Creek (Stawell) in 1866 with gold mines on a ridge in the background. The building on the right with the awning is the office of the *Ararat Advertiser* of which John Bezer Drew was a representative. Picture painted by Robert Watchorn (Cover of *The Golden Years of Stawell*), from a photograph.

Upper Main Street, Pleasant Creek, 1866

In 1863, the family was still in Pleasant Creek (Stawell) where Susan Drew, another daughter was born, but later died aged 3 weeks. An entry for 1864 gives the birth of a further daughter, Susan Drew, who died at the age of 2 days.

The years of 1865 and 1866 had produced another move, this time to Carlton, a suburb of Melbourne, 150 miles from Stawell. Another son, William Drew, was born there in 1865 but died after three days. The following year, 1866, Frank Drew was born on the 20 September also in Carlton, with John Bezer Drew now listed as a Hawker.

Yet another move to the suburb of Emerald Hill (now South Melbourne) was made probably in 1867, where Susan Clara Drew was born at 18 Little York Street, on the 15 June 1868. John Bezer Drew gave his occupation as a General Dealer.

The poor quality photograph illustrated below shows the family at their home, probably 80 Coventry Street, Emerald Hill, circa 1870.

John Bezer Drew and family at their residence in Emerald Hill, Melbourne
From right to left: John Bezer Drew; Wife, Elizabeth Drew;
Son, Thomas Bezer Drew; Elizabeth Charlotte Drew with Susan in front;
Amelia Bezer Caroline Drew; John Drew; Frank Drew.

The family was now to remain permanently in the Melbourne vicinity, and another child, Ada Drew was born in 1871, but died aged 1 day.

From this time John Bezer Drew became busily involved in public affairs, both of a social and political nature. He had been active in the Chartist scene up to the time he left England, and now that he had settled in Melbourne, his radical interests became more prominent.

In 1872, he was a member of the Democratic Association of Victoria, and a committee member of the Melbourne Eclectic Association. In 1874, he became a member of the Constitutional Reform League, as well as a member of the Workingmen's Political Association.

During that year he gave several lectures, commencing with 'A Political Creed for the Coming Election' that he presented to The Sunday Free Discussion Society at the Trades Hall, Carlton, on 28 February. This was followed on the 5 May by 'Women of the Bible' for the Free Thought Debating Society – with a second lecture by request on the 23 May - continuing with 'The Autobiography of John Stuart Mill' on the 27 June.

On the 10 October he lectured on 'The Comparative Merits of Deism and Atheism', and on the 26 December he presented 'The Fourth Commandment' at the Free Thought Discussion Society.

He continued in a similar vein throughout 1875, becoming a member of the Progressive Land Tax League, the Victorian Protection League and a committee member of the Total Abstinence Society, Melbourne, from 1875 –1877.

Through 1875, he continued lecturing for the Free Thought Discussion Society. On the 20 March his subject was ' The Bible's Idol' followed by 'Fear God and Honor the King' on the 17 July.

A sample of his public speaking was reported by the *Melbourne Daily Telegraph* of the 15 October 1875 from a lecture he gave at the Eastern Market, the previous day. His style was reminiscent of his oratory during the Chartist days, examples of which were given in Part One:

'... Politics and political science should be essentially the study of the workingman. The large landowners and other wealthy monopolists had hitherto governed this colony and had taken care to look after their own interests to the injury of the masses. And it was time for the older men like himself who knew the poverty that existed in England among millions of people through the monopoly of a few to say to the young men of this colony: "Wake up! or the abuses of the old country will come on you!" (loud cheering). The unholy league of conspirators against the Berry Government had said that they would give the people more than Mr Berry had promised, but he ventured to assert that their career would be a perpetuation of swindling.

Notwithstanding the importance of Protection the great subject for the people to address themselves to now was that of a land tax so that the wealthy should bear their fair share of the burden of taxation, and therefore he could not see anything more just than the progressive land tax of John Woods.' [John Woods was the Member for Murat in the Legislative Assembly and a friend or acquaintance from the 1860's.]

On the 10 November 1875, he became a foundation member of the Spiritualist and Free Thought Association.

During 1876 he continued with his Association work, as well as joining the National Reform League, concerning which and the government of the time he wrote a letter - with some of his old recognisable radical chartist fire - to the editor of the *Melbourne Age* newspaper:

'Sir – On the 10th April, 1848, a petition signed – even according to the authorised report of the appointed reviewers – by at least a million and a half of men, was presented to the English House of Commons, having for one of its objects the enactment of Annual Parliaments: and your issue of today, exactly twenty-eight years afterwards, and published, some fourteen thousand miles from Trafalgar Square, advocates the same measure for the colony. So in this particular instance, and by a singular coincidence "History Repeats Itself". As your humble servant happened to be one of the "Ragamuffins" of that date, will you permit me a word in your valuable paper:

Long before what is termed, the present crisis, and before indeed, payment of members became law, I urged at several public and other meetings the advisability of annual parliaments on principle: and surely, now we are cursed with an assembly of worse than incapable – blackguard, drunkard and unprincipled – headed by a traitor leader, and defying public opinion repeatedly and unmistakably expressed, the people will wake up to the fact that one year is quite long enough to be insulted and pleaded by people whom we handsomely pay to represent us forsooth.

If yearly parliaments had been the law of the land, the scandalous proceedings of the last few months would never have been attempted. The National Reform League should take this important subject up. I breached the matter at their last meeting, but there was no visible response. Now however "The Age" has spoken with no uncertain mood, let me venture to hope that all good Democrats will rally to the cry. An organised agitation should at once commence, and no candidate returned at the next election unless he pledges himself to support this (as our painful experience proves) necessary measure.

Annual parliaments will soon reform the Assembly, and a reformed Assembly will soon reform the Council. The old motto "Short reckonings make long friends" appears to apply as aptly to politicians as it does to commercial place actions; more especially as our government men evidently consider politics more governing for place and pay.

Very well gentlemen, you pay yourselves most unblushingly, and just as if you had paid yourselves once every month. So from henceforth present yourselves once every year to your employers. If you have been good and faithful, you will be most assuredly and gladly, aye and gratefully be re-engaged: but if unprofitable, go as we will have you no more.
Yours &
Emerald Hill. 10th April. J.B. Drew.'

Victoria was the first of the Australian colonies in 1870 to introduce payment of Members of Parliament. Graham Berry became Premier of Victoria in August 1875 but retired the following October when Sir James McCulloch assumed office. The General Election in 1877 saw Graham Berry again appointed. There was political instability for many years, with clashes between the Legislative Council and the Legislative Assembly.

Following his foundation membership of the Spiritualist and Free Thought Association in 1875, John Bezer Drew was appointed Secretary of the Association on the 23 April 1876. That year also, another daughter died – Amelia Bezer Caroline Drew aged 14 died from Typhoid Fever on 3 March at Emerald Hill.

Some of the lectures that he presented for the Association during 1876 had strong religious titles as well as political connotations:

'Satan in Parliament' on 12 February;
'The Holy Religion of Spiritualism' at the Masonic Hall on the 11 March;
'Resurrection of Christ' on the 15 April, and
'A Bungling Bundle of Bothering Old Letters', 6 August.

Despite his radical opinions, he had remained basically true to the religious views that he had developed during his early 'Dissenting' days.

In March 1878, Australia was stirred by the news of extreme heroism. A ship named the 'Loch Ard' travelled from Gravesend, England, to Port Phillip, Melbourne, with cargo, and 54 passengers and crew. Resulting from bad weather, the ship was off course, struck a small island near the Australian coastline and sank. Only two persons survived; Eva Carmichael aged 18 and a 19 year old Midshipman, Tom Pearce. Pearce found the girl clinging to a spar, and took an hour to swim with her to the shore. Staying in a cave with her overnight, the following day he walked 2 miles to summon help, and returned to Eva at the cave until rescuers arrived.

John Bezer Drew was also impressed with this account of heroism, and composed a descriptive poem to champion the hero, Tom Pearce. He published this – by request – and it was placed on sale priced One Penny.

TOM PEARCE,
The HERO of the Loch Ard.

"Avast there, and don't make Tom proud,
    To be sure, I was brave and what not;
And am pleas'd with your plaudits so loud,
    But you pile up your praise such a lot.
God be praised for my precious good luck,
    'Twas He gave me courage to save,
Thank heav'n for my strength and my pluck
    That snatch'd *one* from a watery grave.

Who would not have tried as I tried?
    My Captain, my shipmates, each one;
Those unfortunate heroes who died,
    Had they lived would have done as I done.
And even the passengers too,
    The sailors to boot, aye, and all;
I know that Miss Eva's true blue.
    And would'nt have shrunk at my call.

A tear for the loved, who are lost,
    A tear for the sadly bereft;
What agony, while tempest tost,
    What agony, too, for those left.
The mothers, the sisters, the wives,

Ah! who can depicture their woe;
As they hear of the sweet priceless lives
　　Swept away by one terrible blow.

Aye, boys. 'twas a dreary long night,
　　For each moment anxiety brought;
As we looked out for land and for light,
　　Prayers, mingled with hopes, that were nought.
She struck on the ridge of a rock,
　　The life boats were got out, but ah,
No avail, for the waves seemed to mock
　　Every effort a poor soul to spare.
The papers will tell you the rest,
　　An Australian's *not* given to *blow*;
I am saved, I am happy, I'm blest,
　　Both saved, and a Saviour I know.
I thank you for all you have thought,
　　For all you have said and have done;
But my duty I did as I ought,
　　I plunged for *her* life and I *won*."

―――――――――

'Tis all mighty fine, Sailor lad,
　　Your estimate thus of an act;
Of your modesty, we are right glad,
　　But your bravery stands as a fact.
And we cannot, will not forbear,
　　Tho' your conscience we feel is your need.
We must tell the when and the where
　　You performed so heroic a deed.

All honour to Pearce then we cry,
　　To *Tom* Pearce belonging to *us*;
Who dared thus to *do*, or to *die*.
　　We'll praise him in prose and in verse.
For his, and her welfare, we pray,
　　Long life and all joy to the two;
But for *him*, an especial huzza!
　　Tom Pearce, the Australian true blue.

　　　　　　　DREW, Emerald Hill.

Published by request – Price One Penny.

John Bezer Drew ca. 1880. Blind in left eye due to smallpox as a child

Elizabeth Bezer Drew ca. 1880

From the early 1880's, John Bezer Drew had become increasingly religious. His daughter, Susan Clara Drew, had married and joined the Salvation Army, becoming Major Barker. The following very orthodox item is from *The Salvation War* (Victoria) 1883 and can be compared to his own account as given in his biography and events noted prior to his move to Australia:

'John B. Drew is an old man sixty-eight years of age, whose conversion to God is another proof of the boundless love of our wonderful Saviour. For forty-five years he had never bowed a knee to God; but, instead, had been "a blasphemer, and a persecutor, and injurious." But "the grace of our Lord was exceeding abundant with faith and love, which is in Christ Jesus" "Howbeit for this cause he obtained mercy, that in him Jesus Christ might show forth all long suffering for a pattern to them which should hereafter believe on Him to life everlasting." Thank God, the once infidel lecturer is now a humble child of God. When a young man, he was a teacher, then superintendent, of a Sunday-school, and a missionary to the Thames seamen.

His mother was a godly woman, but his father was a drunken sailor. His minister was a proud young aristocrat, without the fear of God in his heart. He induced young Drew and a few more of his congregation to be immersed; and as they had no baptistry in their chapel the minister borrowed a Unitarian chapel, and instead of the usual address on adult baptism, he made an attack upon the Unitarians who had loaned their chapel. This brought up rejoinders, and young Drew and his companions went to hear the Unitarian defence. They subsequently waited upon their own minister for information upon doctrines which were assailed by the Unitarians; but instead of tender dealing and clear teaching they were turned out with denunciations. Two went off at once to infidel lecture-rooms, while young Drew sought for ease to his troubled mind by attending every church or chapel he could get in to until he was chained up by Giant Despair; then he often contemplated suicide. He took to drink, theatres, gambling-houses, and mixed up with every ism save atheism. With hot tears he would often quote the words at his baptism –

When any turn from Zion's ways –
Alas! what numbers do! –
I think I hear my Saviour say,
"Wilt thou forsake Me too?"

There was unrest and sometimes despair; but there was no real repentance, no real prayer to God, no pleading for mercy, no prostration at the cross. It was all human reason and argumentation. Years passed on, and the Chartist agitation began. Drew was then a political and infidel stump orator. In 1848, for a speech not according to law, he received a sentence of two years in Newgate, with eighteen months solitary confinement.

When liberated, he had to find bail for three years' good behaviour; but this was soon forfeited through publishing a leading article in a newspaper. He had to flee from England. [Note: No article traced. But see pages 50, 54, 137. Ed.] He came to Australia, and, according to his own statement, has been a willing slave of the devil; "even *he*, surely, might be satisfied with forty-five years undisguised treason against the King of kings."

He threw himself as an energetic worker into the band of public blasphemers, and for has been in the front "railing" against Christ. But what led to his conversion? His good wife and daughter were connected with the South Melbourne Corps, and they invited him to the Salvation Army. But that he scorned -
"A philosopher go to the Salvation Army! to look at a lot of lunatics and fools?" But they pressed him frequently, and for peace sake he went three times to the South Melbourne and twice to Collingwood. Good people asked him if he were saved.
"No! Didn't want to be their way." Time slipped on, and the New Year's Day demonstrations in the Exhibition was held. His wife took him, and, to quote his own words,

"Merciful God! there were thousands of happy saints there, singing all about Jesus and heaven; not is a Laodicean manner, but singing and meaning it, with their hands and feet, and lungs; ah! and better, with their hearts. Meaning it. Major Barker 'bound for the better land;' but poor me, where was I bound to? O for my Sunday-school again! O for the old-time religion again!"

That night I spent in bitter agony; nevertheless not repentant, but savage. The next morning, at about nine o'clock, the blessed Lord laid hold on me, and down on my knees I wept and prayed with groanings which cannot be uttered, my dear wife and child at mercy's throne pleading. [Perhaps a thought of his bigamous marriage? Ed.] The enemy said,

'You think of mercy; why, you fool, you have committed the unpardonable sin – the sin against the Holy Ghost. You can't be pardoned; go and get drunk; or do as Judas did!'

But I did neither. No more drink, no more sin; damned or not damned, if I have to go to hell I'll just go praying - praying to the last gasp. So the sad day wore on, and the night and all the next day, until the Friday afternoon. The last prayer I uttered was, perhaps, the strangest ever made by a broken-down sinner. I remember it well –

'O trampled-on Christ! Just pardon me, or *don't*; only *do* tell, or I shall go stark mad!"

A few moments after that semi-blasphemous petition, when I felt that the devil himself would come and damn me, light broke in.

With pitying eyes the Prince of Peace
Beheld my helpless grief;
He saw, and oh! amazing love,
He flew to my relief.

The voice went through my delighted soul, 'Thy sins, which are many, are all forgiven; go, and sin no more!' Gracious pardon full and free! With stern command at once the wonderful Word of my neglected, despised, rejected Jesus came with a mighty power, and the precious blood was applied. 'How precious did that Christ appear the hour I first believed!' Leaping up for very joy I shouted,

'Betty, I'm saved! Yes, saved; even me, saved! He has abundantly pardoned! Hallelujah!' '

John Bezer Drew died on the 12 January 1888 aged 71, following a stroke a fortnight earlier, at his daughter's home at Moray Place, South Melbourne. His occupation was given as a 'Bill-poster.' He was buried at Carlton Old Melbourne Cemetery. Grave, Wesleyan Methodist F 705. There is no headstone. His wife, Elizabeth Drew aged 65, died on the 9 January 1894 from Tuberculosis at her daughter's home at Penshurst, Victoria.

Of his surviving children, John Bezer Drew's first son, Thomas Bezer Drew became a noted political figure, representing North Ward

Ratepayers for 21 years. Elected twice as a Councillor, he became Mayor from 1913-1914 and from 1924-1925, retiring in 1933.

His second son, John Drew, was an active member of the Protectionist Association of Victoria (created 1894), that aimed in general to promote industries and assist workers by means of a protective tariff.

John Drew (John Bezer Drew's second son) c. 1900

This completes to date, the biographical information that is available concerning John James Bezer (Drew). Although the major events in his life have now been recorded, some queries remain, as noted in Part One.

a) At the baptism of Emily Drew Bezer on 12 October 1859, her parents were listed as John James Bezer and Jane Sarah Bezer of 9 Orchard Place, Shoreditch.

But in Australia, Mary Burl Drew was born in Ararat on the 22 December 1859, and John Drew signed as the informant on the 31 December.

b) According to the census record for 6 April 1861, Bezer was listed then as being at 2A Old Bethnal Green Road, with his wife, Jane, and two children.

However, John Bezer Drew's daughter, Mary, had died in Ararat on the 1 February 1861 from Whooping Cough after five weeks illness. The informant was John Drew, Shoemaker, who registered it on the same date.

Also for the birth of Amelia Bezer Caroline Drew in Pleasant Creek on the following 21 September 1861, John Bezer Drew was the informant – albeit with some delay - on the 12 November.

It is therefore impossible that John James Bezer (Drew) could have been in London on the date of Emily Drew Bezer's baptism. It is also impossible that Bezer could have travelled the slow and long distance from Ararat to London in the nine weeks between the 1 February and the 6 April 1861, the date of the census. The sea journey alone would take between 10 and 17 weeks at that time.

Lord Goderich had tracked Bezer to Australia, and presumably received some knowledge of his remarriage that was passed on to John Ludlow. A number of chartists had already emigrated to the Australian goldfields. These included Henry Holyoake, the brother of George Jacob Holyoake who, in 1853 was responsible with George Black, a radical Chartist, for commencing in Melbourne, a paper *The Digger's Advocate*. Information may have been obtained via them. It would appear strange if Bezer's wife and family had not also learned of it. Emily Drew Bezer's marriage certificate dated 1868, as quoted earlier, gave John Bezer as 'Deceased." Assuming that the 7-year Presumption of Death of a missing person is taken into account, it is very likely that Bezer's wife had obtained a surrogate, and would confirm that Bezer had never returned to England. No remarriage, death certificate or later census record of Jane

Sarah Bezer has been found following her witnessing the marriage of Bezer's son, Francis James, in November 1862.

More material concerning the literary life of John Bezer (Drew) should certainly be available in local newspapers of the period where he lectured in England, and also in Australian newspapers to which he corresponded.

Remaining a staunch radical from his early Chartist days, he continued in a similar idealistic manner in Australia by both lecturing and writing, although much of his old fire had mellowed. Nevertheless, he undoubtedly left his mark both in England and Australia by influencing local opinion. Perhaps if he had been less restless and prepared to settle for longer periods, he would have developed and focussed his sound literary abilities to a greater and more positive extent. However, he will certainly remain as an interesting outspoken reformist, his writings and reports of his oratory reflecting most effectively a particular political and social tone of his age.

References:

Golden Years of Stawell, by Robert Murray and Kate White, Lothian Publishing Co. Pty. Ltd, Melbourne, 1983.

History of Postal Services in Victoria. Christine Gibbs, Australia Post, 1984.

John Ludlow. The Autobiography of a Christian Socialist, ed. A. Murray, London, 1981.

Life of the First Marquess of Ripon, by Lucien Wolf, London, 1921.

Melbourne Age, as cited.

Melbourne Daily Telegraph, as cited.

The Salvation War. Victoria, Australia, 1883.

See also the biography of Gerald Massey.

Acknowledgements to Norman W. Drew of Victoria, Australia.

JOHN ARNOTT
1799 – 1868

GENERAL SECRETARY
THE NATIONAL CHARTER ASSOCIATION

1

POLITICS AND POETRY

There has been no portrait or physical description recorded, and there is little information available concerning the personal life of John Arnott, noted for being sometime Secretary and General Secretary of the National Charter Association. His name comes down to us principally in the reports of meetings of the National Charter Association, and other associated organisations with which he was involved during a period from the mid 1840's to mid 1850's. Details of the particular events together with their background can readily be traced in the relevant Chartist newspapers and books on Chartist history.

It is probably safe to infer that John Arnott joined the National Charter Association soon after its inception in 1840. His progress within the organisation was rapid, and he was highly regarded and respected for his efficiency. However, there is no record of him undertaking lecturing or article writing that would have brought his name to a more prominent position in the Chartist press, although he did compose some poems that were published in the *Northern Star*. From 1853 and the virtual death of the Chartist movement, he is unrecorded. It appears that he, together with many other official stalwarts gave up that particular struggle, and supported associated organisations, or continued with their own personal affairs.

John Arnott was born on the 22 October 1799, at Chesham, Bucks, the son of William and Mary Arnott. There were another three sons and two daughters in the family, all born in Chesham, between 1802 and 1807. George, born 29 April 1802; Elizabeth, born 1 December 1804; Joseph and Benjamin (twins) born September 1807.

Dust heaps. Somers Town, 1836
The building in the background is the London Small pox and Fever Hosiptal.
This was demolished in the 1840's to make way for the building of King's Cross
Railway Station.

On the 19 October 1819, he married Sarah Allen at Chesham Bois. It appears that he resided in Chesham until 1830 – 1835, when the family moved to London.

Census records for 1841 show him residing at Suters Buildings, St Pancras, with his wife and six children – Alfred 15, b. Chesham. Ann 13, b. Chesham. Benjamin 11, b. Chesham. Emma 4, Sarah 2, and Edwin 4 months b. St Pancras. John Arnott is listed there as a 'Cordwainer' [Shoemaker]. Suters Buildings appear to have been situated in Somers Town in an area between Ossulston Street, Middlesex Street, Phoenix Street and Chapel Street. Today, now redeveloped, between Ossulston Street and Brill Place, behind the British Library.

Arnott obviously made steady progress within the National Charter Association. In 1844, he was a member of the Somers Town Branch of the Metropolitan Delegate Council. On the 8 June (*Northern Star*) at a meeting of the Council he moved that a national petition be got up by each locality praying for the deliverance of Thomas Cooper, now confined in Stafford Gaol. On the 3 August, he took the Chair at a Delegate Council meeting, and on October 5 at a Council meeting, he was elected Secretary. His address at that time was given as Middlesex Place, Somers Town.

On December 10 1844, a well attended soiree was held at the Literary Institute, John Street, in honour of the removal of the *Northern Star* from Leeds to London. George Julian Harney, Feargus O'Connor and other leaders were present, and gave many toasts and strong addresses. John Arnott sang a patriotic song amidst considerable applause. On January 18 1845, he was elected Secretary of the Delegate Council with re-election on the 13 May for a further three months.

On the 19 March his eldest son, Alfred, at 8c Middlesex Place, Somers Town, married Eliza Cavell of the same address. Eliza's father listed as a labourer.

The following year, 1846, was a year of great cheer for the Chartists. Feargus O'Connor had been preparing his Co-operative Land Society for a launch that, he anticipated, would place the Chartists at the forefront of land co-operative for impoverished workers. Many of the prominent Chartists supported the venture, including Ernest Jones. John Arnott also gave his support, and provided a poem that he composed especially for the occasion.

This was an over optimistic eulogy for the opening celebration of O'Connor's ill-fated Society (The National Land Company) to be held on the 17 August 1846. The People's First Estate (the first of six purchased and plots issued by shares) was some 100 acres located at

Heronsgate, near Rickmansworth, and was known as 'O'Connorville.' It had 35 specially designed properties for cheap rent, and a schoolhouse. (See *The Chartist Land Company*, A.M. Hadfield, David & Charles 1970, p.101.) The poem was printed and placed on sale at the site on opening day, priced 1d.

Northern Star, August 1 1846, p.3.

Songs for the People xxiv.

The People's First Estate,
Or, Anticipation of the 17th August.

Air,- "The days that we went gipsying."

Come let us leave the murky gloom,
    The narrow crowded street;
The bustle, noise, the smoke and din;
    To breathe the air that's sweet.
We'll leave the gorgeous palaces,
    To those miscalled great;
To spend a day of pleasure on
    The People's First Estate!
CHORUS, - *On this estate the sons of toil*
    Shall independent be,
    Enjoy the first fruits of the soil,
    From tyranny set free!

The banners waving in the breeze,
    The bands shall cheerfully play,
Let all be mirth and holiday
    On this our holiday
Unto the farm – "O'Connorville,"
    That late was "Herringsgate,"
We go to take possession of
    The People's First Estate!
    On this estate, etc.

When on the farm! The People's Farm!
    This land of liberty!
We'll join the dances and rural games,
    With joy and sportive glee,

Our gambols play, throughout the day,
    (To scoffers you may prate,)
And leave at night this lovely scene,
    The People's First Estate!
      On this estate, etc.

May nature shed her choicest stores,
    On this delightful spot;
Each occupant be blest indeed,
    And peace attend each cot.
And may our brave Directors with
    The funds that we'll create,
Live long to purchase hundreds more
    Like this our first estate!
      On our estate the sons of toil
      Shall independent be;
      Enjoy the first fruits of the soil,
      From tyranny set free!

John Arnott
Somers Town
July 27 1846.

Arnott had earlier composed a poem for the occasion of the First Annual Festival to celebrate the anniversary of the French Republic. This was held at the White Conduit Tavern on April 21 1846, but the poem was not printed in the *Northern Star* until some time later:

Northern Star, 19 September 1846, p. 5.

Songs for the People no. xxx

A SONG ADDRESSED TO THE FRATERNAL DEMOCRATS

AIR - "Auld Lang Syne"

All hail, Fraternal Democrats,
    Ye friends of Freedom hail,
Whose noble object is - that base
    Despotic power shall fail.

Chorus - That mitres, thrones, misrule and wrong,
   Shall from this earth be hurled,
  And peace, goodwill, and brotherhood,
   Extend throughout the world.
Associated to proclaim
   The equal rights of man.
Progression's army! firm, resolved,
   On! forward lead the van.
      Till mitres, thrones, misrule and wrong,
         Shall from this earth be hurled.
      And peace, goodwill, and brotherhood,
         Extend throughout the world.

To aid this cause we here behold,
   British and French agree,
Spaniard and German, Swiss and Pole,
   With joy the day would see.
      When mitres, thrones, misrule, and wrong,
         Will from this earth be hurled,
      And peace, goodwill, and brotherhood,
         Extend throughout the world.

We now are met to celebrate
   The deeds of spirits brave,
Who struggled, fought, and bled, and died,
   Their misrul'd land to save.
      For mitres, thrones, misrule and wrong,
         From France they nobly hurled,
      And would have spread Democracy
         Throughout this sea-girt world.

Though kings and priests might then combine
   To crush sweet liberty,
We tell them now that they must bow,
   That man shall yet be free.
      That mitres, thrones, misrule and wrong,
         Shall from this earth be hurled,
      And peace, goodwill, and brotherhood,
         Extend throughout the world.

Oh! may that period soon arrive,
   When kings will cease to be,
And freedom and equality

144

Extend from sea to sea.
　　Then mitres, thrones, misrule and wrong,
　　　Will from this earth be hurled,
　　And peace, goodwill, and brotherhood,
　　　Shall reign throughout the world.

John Arnott
Somers Town, September 1846

The poem was followed by a similar stirring piece by George Julian Harney, titled 'All Men are Brethren'. A song for the Fraternal Democrats.

Appreciative, as many were, of the hard work and dedication showed by Ernest Jones, Arnott then composed a poem in his honour, in the form of an acrostic:

Northern Star 17 October 1846, p.3.

AN ACROSTIC

To Ernest Jones, Esq., Barrister-at-Law

Estranged Aristocrat! What leave the favoured few,
Regardless of fortune and prospects in view,
(Noble Democrat) to join the Chartist band,
Eschewed, despised, and scouted through the land.
Such conduct we esteem, nay more, admire,
Thy spirit burns with freedom's sacred fire.
Just as the trav'ler pursuing his lonely way,
On whose dark path meteors bursting play,
Now changing gloom to bright refulgent day;
Ernest we hail thee, from thy genius bright
Shines in full power pure Democratic light.

John Arnott
Somers Town.
Oct. 12th 1846.

[Note: The first letter of each line forms the name 'Ernest Jones'.]

The following year Arnott composed yet another poem to honour Thomas Slingsby Duncombe (1796 – 1861) MP for Finsbury, who had petitioned for the release of imprisoned Chartists in 1842. Duncombe was also sympathetic towards Louis Kossuth and Guiseppe Mazzini. Mazzini, exiled in England, had the aim of promoting Italian unity, republicanism and democracy. He was suspected by the government of being a participant in organising an attempt at an invasion of Italy, and Sir James Graham, Home Secretary authorised the opening of Mazzini's letters.

Northern Star, March 13 1847, p.3.

A SONG
(Air – with Helmet on his Brow)
In honour of that indomitable friend and advocate of the Rights of Labour, T.S. Duncombe, MP.

> Let the base sycophant
>   Of wars and heroes sing;
> 'Laud the despot' cringe and bow
>   To Emperor or King:
> I scorn such fulsome themes,
>   I sing of the patriot brave,
> Duncombe, the friend of Liberty,
>   And Labour's worn-down slave.

> *CHORUS.- Let all as one smite,*
>   *And join in freedom's cause,*
>   *Shouting for "Duncombe and our Right;*
>   *Free, just, and equal laws!"*
> When the Whigs and Tories join'd
>   The Labourer to enslave,
> Duncombe crush'd their monster Bill,
>   And consigned it to its grave.
> The Post-office espionage
>   Pursued in Graham's plan,
> Duncombe did nobly upset,
>   And exposed that hateful man.
> Let all as one, etc.

The poor in Bastilles doomed
　　Their wretched lives to spend, -
The toiling slaves – the factory child –
　　Duncombe has been their friend;
He has their wrongs denounced,
　　He will their rights demand,
And labour would emancipate
　　From the grasping tyrant hand.
Let all as one, etc.

He will defend the oppressed,
　　The Irish or the Pole;
The deeds of despots are deplor'd
　　By his patriotic soul.
Duncombe they cannot bribe –
　　He's honest firm and bold,
And, as the leader of our cause,
　　His worth cannot be told.
Let all as one, etc.

Let the Tories talk of Peel,
　　The Whigs of Russell boast,
Duncombe is our champion,
　　And this shall be our toast: -
"To Duncombe and the Trades,
　　Duncombe and Liberty;
To Duncombe and the Charter,
　　And may we soon be free!"
　　　　Let all as one smite,
　　　　　And join in freedom's cause,
　　　　Shouting for "Duncombe and our Right;
　　　　　Free, just, and equal laws!"

John Arnott.
Somers Town.

Until the virtual demise of the National Charter Association, the ensuing years were busy for John Arnott. In August 1846 he had taken the Chair at the first Amalgamated Meeting of the chartist's Veterans, Orphans and Victim Relief Committee, and at a public meeting in October at St Pancras on 'The Charter and no surrender', he read and moved the adoption of the National Petition. In the same month he was elected a member of the Fraternal Democrats, when he was referred to at that time as the 'Somers Town Chartist Rhymer.'

In October he was appointed Assistant Secretary to the Veterans, Orphans and Victim Committee, and in November at the South London Chartist Hall, he was Sub-Secretary. During the following month his poetry was again noted, and he was mentioned then as "our respected and indefatigable sub-secretary, Rhyming John Arnott." His address was given as 8 Middlesex Street, Somers Town.

Considerable prominence was being given in the following year to the Chartist petition that was to be presented to Parliament in April 1847. This publicity caused fears of violence, and a pseudonymous letter was published in the *Times* of 1 April in which the writer quoted an announcement by 'Vernon' made at a recent Chartist meeting. In this, mention was made of an intended procession of between 100,000 to 300,000 persons. The writer of the letter queried protection of the rights of shopkeepers against the 'tumultuous proceedings,' and that suspension of their business appeared to be an infliction and a robbery.

This letter was brought to the attention of the Chartist Committee appointed to deal with the arrangements of the demonstration on the 10 April.

John Arnott, as Secretary, was requested to repudiate in the strongest terms the language thus ascribed to have been uttered by Mr Vernon, and to state most emphatically that it was the "firm determination of the committee that the demonstration shall be a peaceable, orderly, and moral display of the unenfranchised toiling masses." (*Times*, 4 April 1848.)

Arnott's address was given as 11 Middlesex Place, Somers Town.

CHARTIST DEMONSTRATION.

TO THE EDITOR OF THE TIMES.

Sir,—At a meeting of the committee appointed by the various metropolitan districts (consisting of 73 delegates) to arrange and carry out the Chartist demonstration on Monday next, April 10, a communication in your paper of Saturday last, relative to the Chartist demonstration, was brought under discussion, when it was resolved, with only one dissentient, that a note be forwarded by the secretary to *The Times* newspaper for insertion, repudiating in the strongest terms the language there ascribed to have been uttered by Mr. Vernon, and also to state most emphatically that it is the firm determination of the committee that the demonstration shall be a peaceable, orderly, and moral display of the unenfranchised and toiling masses.

Trusting that you will insert this in your next journal,

I am, Sir, yours most respectfully,

JOHN ARNOTT, Secretary.

11, Middlesex-place, Somers-town, April 3.

On the 24 March, Arnott, on behalf of he National Victim and Defence Committee (assumed to be the Relief Committee as previously mentioned) made a request for more financial contributions. He noted that the law made widows and nearly 100 orphans plus the wives and families of Ernest Jones, Peter McDouall and others dependent on support. Giving 3 shillings each to the widows and one shilling for every child under 12, left the Committee liabilities of £10 p.w. That week, two shillings only could be afforded to a woman with 5, 6, or 7 children for seven days.

In August, it was reported that the balance sheet over 17 weeks showed receipts as £103, expenditure £102. This amount was divided amongst 31 families (30 grown persons and 70 children), and Arnott made a further appeal the following month.

London branches of the NCA met on a regular basis to discuss general and local issues – and it appears that some of the proposals were destined only to give verbal support to the overall cause. On the 31 March 1849 Arnott seconded a Resolution 'that the present so-called representation of the people is a monstrous injustice on the nation at large, and a violation of the British Constitution.' About this time, it was realised that it would be an advantage if local groups could cohese and provide general unity within the movement. At a meeting of the General Registration and Election Committee, Arnott and another member proposed that a Hand-Book and Guide to Regulations and Elections be published at two pence a copy, and that the Chartist Executive be requested to aid circulation. The Metropolitan District Council to consist of two members from each locality within the metropolis and suburbs, and to cause a fusion of all whom advocate Chartist Suffrage, into one united phalanx.

July 1850 was the month that Ernest Jones was released from prison. He was met by John Arnott and several others, and the next day the Fraternal Democrats gave a supper in his honour. Arnott, G.W.M. Reynolds, Bronterre O'Brien, George Julian Harney and others proposed toasts in his honour. Testimonials were presented, together with a pair of large portraits of Mr and Mrs Jones. The following day, there was a public meeting at the John Street Institute in honour of Jones' release. Harney took the Chair, with the Executive of the NCA on the platform, and Walter Cooper, Reynolds and others gave addresses.

Later that month, the NCA Executive met with a view of reuniting the NCA, Fraternal Democrats and National Reform League into one body. The name suggested was the National Charter Association Federal Union – later agreed to be National Charter and Social Reform Union. This inevitably received a mixed reception, and caused ongoing dissent.

On the 27 November 1850, the NCA Executive Committee resigned, and votes were taken for another Executive. The General Secretary was to be paid, while the Executive was unpaid. Arnott was elected to the Executive, and later was confirmed as General Secretary, thus replacing Samuel Kydd who was receiving a salary of £2 per month.

The 1851 census return for 11 Middlesex Place, Somers Town, gives: John Arnott, 51. Cordwainer, b. Chesham. Sarah Arnott, 51, b. Bovington, Herts. Benjamin, 21, Brush finisher. Emma, 14. Sarah, 12. Edwin, 10.

Arnott's son, Benjamin, was married on the 13 April 1851 at Trinity Church, St Andrew to Eleanor Wilmott, of Middlesex Place. Her father, like Arnott, was also a Shoemaker, and the couple went to live at 9 Brill Place, Somers Town.

Differences of opinion concerning the best way to promote the Chartist movement were becoming more acute in that period. At a meeting of the NCA on the 19 March 1851, Arnott and Ernest Jones proposed a long stirring address for unity, to be read at locality meetings.

The main drive of the address, similar to one given as at a meeting the previous year, was to unite disparate organisations in one phalanx. 'Henceforth let social co-operation go hand in hand with political organisation... Unite! unite! unite! The convention must be the PARLIAMENT OF LABOUR! The Executive, the MINISTRY OF THE UNENFRANCHISED!'

Some of the Districts were also becoming opposed to the leaders of the National Charter Association, with John Arnott also subject to displeasure. In the *Northern Star* of 22 March 1851, Arnott responded via the Editor to criticisms made by the Radford locality in a postscript item in the previous issue. He replied:

> "...the postscript runs thus- 'We have frequently seen notices from the Executive, stating that correspondence had been received from Radford and other places complaining of their inability to send delegates. So far as we are concerned, we deny such a statement.'
>
> Now, Sir, being of opinion that the above is calculated to damage the Executive, and to impress the idea on the public mind that I, as their secretary, have published FALSE REPORTS, I, therefore, feel it to be my duty, in reply thereto, to state that I have minutely examined the printed reports for the last eight weeks, and I must say that Mr. Brown has superior penetration to what I possess, as I cannot find Radford therein mentioned, consequently, I request Mr. Brown to point to the reports to which he alludes, and, failing doing so, I shall leave it for our readers to decide which has published a false statement, Mr. Brown or myself..."

In another instance, it had been agreed earlier that the Metropolitan Delegate Committee's meetings would include representatives from the NCA Executive. For some reason, these did not turn up a meeting held in December. A report in the *Northern Star* for 20 December 1851 concerning the election of a new NCA Executive expressed the displeasure of one locality:

> Finsbury Locality. Report from the Metropolitan Delegate Committee: "That this locality consider the absence of the whole of the Executive from the Metropolitan Delegate Committee meeting as deserving of explanation; and the General Secretary is deserving of censure, seeing that it was his duty to have attended the aforesaid meeting. The locality recommend the new Executive to elect as their General Secretary a man of known ability and straightforward conduct and able to address Public Meetings, and that we recommend

Thomas Martin Wheeler – seeing that the inefficiency of the late General Secretary is a matter of public notoriety and regret."

It would appear that Arnott, who had family responsibilities and relied for his living as a shoemaker, acted principally as an administrator and could not afford the time to lecture, even locally. Lecture tours often demanded a considerable amount of time away, with some expenses not always reimbursed. On this account Arnott was, therefore, considered a less active participant than Thomas Wheeler. However, apparently neither the NCA nor Arnott responded to the remarks made by the locality.

In early January 1852, the new Executive Committee had their first meeting, during which dissention became even more apparent. Harney had declined to stand for election, believing that the NCA was virtually finished. Arnott was present, with John James Bezer in the Chair. Arnott read a letter from W.J. Linton, in which he stated his belief that it was impossible to resuscitate the Chartist movement, and declined to sit on the Executive unless the movement joined the middle class. Ernest Jones resigned. The NCA had for some time developed a strong socialist stance, attempting to unite the Chartists, the Co-operatives and the Trades into one movement. The Manchester Chartist's supporters opposed the NCA. Arnott then read the accounts, revealing a debt of some £37. Unable to pay the Secretary's expenses, it was moved that J.M. Wheeler act as Secretary, but this was not seconded and Wheeler resigned from the Committee. John Arnott then agreed to serve for one month, but two members opposed the nomination, and the Chairman's vote caused his resignation as Secretary, although he remained on the Committee. Other members were nominated, but declined to stand. Finally, James Grassby consented to act as Secretary for one month.

In one of a series of articles in the *Northern Star*, on January 17 1852, a pseudonymous 'Censor', complained that:

"... the charge of the people's cause has fallen into the hands of Messrs Arnott, Bezer, Grassby, Shaw and Holyoake..." and asked "if these are the persons who should be entrusted with the conduct of so important a movement ... knowing how limited were the powers which such persons could bring to the duties they aspired to discharge..."

In broad terms the accusation was correct, as the Executive was ruled by dissention, opposition, and decreasing support from the working classes. Harney had wanted a merger between Chartists, trades unions and co-operatives, whilst Ernest Jones continued to press for the NCA as the sole Chartist organisation. This barely viable NCA lasted until 1858 when it finally ceased to exist.

The apparent inefficiency of the Executive of the NCA was now blamed for the miserable state of the Chartist movement, and Arnott and the Executive complained that the Manchester Council was set up to supersede the NCA. Another meeting referred to the Finsbury Locality having objected to Messrs Le Blond and Thornton Hunt having seats (replacing Linton and Jones). James Grassby in response to the Finsbury Locality's remarks stated that, "We think it a pity that men seeking political power should have such a vague knowledge of how to use it."

On the 27 March 1852 *The Star and National Trades' Journal* reported a meeting of the Executive Committee, when the famous statement was made that it was

"The Executive of a society, almost without members, and without means – members reduced by unwise antagonism without, and influence reduced by repeated resignations within...".

Despite this, it was later agreed that Arnott, Bezer and others were to continue in office (probably only on a temporary basis for three months), and Arnott remained on the Democratic Refugee Committee up to November 1852.

The situation was similar to that of William Lovett's earlier Working Men's Association that had, in October 1836, proposed resolutions towards a viable 'People's Charter'. Thomas Cooper, Feargus O'Connor and George Julian Harney were members for a time, including a number of well known later Chartist activists. In 1849 that Association was in debt, and it was stated that "Cliqueism and dissentions helped to kill that Association, as in other movements." (*A History of the Working Men's Association from 1836 to 1850*, by George Howell, 1900. Published Frank Graham, Newcastle, 1970).

In July 1853 the American and British public were stirred by the news regarding the rescue of Martin Coszta, a Hungarian refugee from an Austrian ship in the port of Smyrna. Coszta was residing in America, and visiting in Smyrna on business. He had stated that he wished to become an American citizen, but was taken by a party of armed Greeks employed by the Austrian consul general, and held on their ship. Captain Duncan Ingraham, commanding a 22 gun sloop-of-war, received permission from the US charge d'affairs in Constantinople to request Coszta's release, or use force to obtain it. This was despite Hungarian ships in the harbour, with firepower greater than Ingraham's. It was then agreed that that Coszta be released to the French consul and from there returned to the United States.

In England, an Ingraham Testimonial Fund Committee was formed, with Arnott as Secretary. The Chairman was G.W.M. Reynolds, with other members that included George Julian Harney, James Grassby, Samuel Kydd, Walter Cooper and Robert Le Blond as Treasurer.

Ingraham was presented with a medal from the US president for Vindicating American Honour, and following the subscription, an inscribed chronometer from the working classes of England.

The 1861 census return for Arnott's last stated address, 11 Middlesex Place, shows it as unoccupied. At the same time, his second eldest son, Benjamin, 30, was residing at 47 Middlesex Street as a 'Licensed Hawker'. His wife, Eleanor, 33, was a laundress, with children Eleanor Diana, 9, Elizabeth Mary, 3, and Clara, 7 months.

John Hollingshead in his *Ragged London 1861* (Smith, Elder), mentions Somers Town as being full of courts and alleys, cheap china shops, cheap clothiers and cheap haberdashers. Wherever there is a butcher's shop, it contrives to look like a cat's-meat warehouse. Its side streets have a smoky, worn-out appearance. Every street door is open, no house is without patched windows and every passage teeming with children. It had a population of some 35,000, and was more industrial than the adjoining Agar Town, between Euston and Kings Cross stations, that was referred to as a disgrace. The Midland Railway cleared Agar Town and part of Somers Town in 1866.

Thomas Martin Wheeler (b. 1811), was a valued Chartist member, author and lecturer. A strong supporter of Feargus O'Connor and his Land Plan, he had purchased a plot at O'Connorville, where he resided for some time. He was elected to the NCA Executive in 1841, and became a popular General Secretary from 1842 to 1846. He died in 1862 and was buried at Highgate Cemetery. Twenty-four horse-drawn carriages followed the hearse to Highgate, accompanied by a large procession. John Arnott, who had supported Wheeler's aims, also attended the funeral.

2

POETRY AND POVERTY

According to W.E. Adams in his *Memoirs of a Social Atom*, chapter xvi,

"Some time about 1865 I was standing at the shop door of a Radical bookseller in the Strand. A poor half-starved old man came to the bookseller, according to custom, to beg or borrow a few coppers. It was John Arnott! Chartism was then, as it really had been for a long time before, a matter of history."

Not long after this, probably in 1866, Arnott suffered a stroke. However, he was able to compose a poem that he sent to Edmund Beales (1803-1881) Chairman of the Reform League, for their forthcoming meeting at the Agricultural Hall, Islington, on 11 February 1867.

As a chartist Arnott had of course supported those activities promoting manhood suffrage and the ballot, and he continued now by the only means available to him – through a poem:

The National Reform League
A Song

Written for the intended Great Reform
on Monday Demonstration
February the 11th 1867

Air "The days that we went gipsying"
By John Arnott Somers Town
1
All hail! Reformers of the League
Ye Friends of Freedom hail
Whose noble object is that base
Despotic power shall fail
Chorus. That Working men shall be esteem'd
No longer "vile and low"
But have the Vote; and Praise the League
As marching on we go

2

The League it will not can not fail
To raise the very low
And fit them in the social scale
As Men who duties know
Chorus. For Working men etc

3

The League has made the Tories quake
By amalgamating mind
Into such full force that very soon
They irresistible will find
Chorus. For Workingmen etc

4

Ye "thousands of" The Reform League
Concentrate all your Powers
Your foes are strong your cause is just
(The front of battle cowers)
Be firm United one and all
The Prize is Liberty
Tell the Tories now that they must bow
That Men will soon be Free
Chorus. For Working men etc

5

So sure as winds the billows dash
Across the foaming Sea
Orbs still roll on and Natures works
In harmony agree
So shall this glorious cause Progress
It can not will not fail
And with such Champions as Beale and Bright
It must it shall prevail
Chorus. For Working men etc

John Arnott
(a Poor Paralysed old chartist)

1 Equity Buildings
Somers Town N.W.
Jan^ry 16th 1867 *

* (Acknowledgements to Bishopsgate Library, Bishopsgate Foundation
and Institute. Ref: Howell/11/2D/131).

The National Reform League
A Song

Written for the intended Great Reform
on Monday February the 11th 1867
Air "The days that are coming bye & bye"
By John Arnett Somers Town

All hail! Reformers of the League
    Ye Friends of Freedom hail
Whose noble object is that base
    Despotic power shall fail

Chorus. That Workingmen shall be esteem'd
            No longer "vile and low"
        But have the Vote; and Praise the League
            As marching on we go ————

2
The League it will not cannot fail
    To raise the very low
And fit them in the social scale
    As Men who Duties know
Chorus   That Workingmen &c

3
The League has made the Tories quake
    By amalgamating mind
Into such full force that very soon
    They irresistable will find
Chorus For Workingmen &c

Ye! Thousands &c of "The Reform League"
Concentrate all your Powers
Your Laws are strong your cause is just
(The front of battle Lowers)
Be firm United one and all
The Prize is Liberty
Tell the Tories now that they must bow
That Men will soon be freemen
Chorus For Workingmen &c

5

So sure as winds the billows dash
Across the foaming Sea
Orbs still roll on and Natures work
In harmony agree
So shall this glorious cause Progress
It cannot will not fail
And with such Champions as Beales and Bright
It must it shall Prevail
Chorus For Workingmen &c
Jan 16th 1867

John Scott
(a Poor Paralyzed Chartist)

Equity Buildings Under Line N.W.

The meeting in Islington commenced with a march from Trafalgar Square, and was represented by a countrywide number of Trade Union brass bands. The *Times* of February 12, p.12 reported that there were no fewer than 30,000 – 60,000 persons in attendance. During the meeting a group called 'The Reform League Minstrels' chanted verses that had been printed, and were then distributed at a penny each, but there is no record of Arnott's poem being made available at the meeting.

On 28 April 1868, John Arnott was admitted to St Pancras Workhouse from his and his wife's residence, at 1, Equity Buildings, Somers Town. He died shortly afterwards on the 6 May of 'Paralysis' [a term for a stroke, at that time], aged 69. This was probably a second stroke following the first 'paralysis' that he mentioned in his letter, which this time proved fatal. His occupation was stated as Shoemaker Journeyman.

St Pancras Workhouse held between 1,500 and 1,900 inmates, of which 200 occupied sick wards, 60 – 70 were lunatics and idiots, and about 1,000 were and Reform League Branches carrying banners and accompanied by helpless infirm and aged. (*Illustrated London News*, 3 October, 1857).

John Arnott was buried on the 12 May in St Pancras Cemetery, High Road, East Finchley, grave no 47, section 10J. The grave was a 'communal' (pauper's) grave, and there is no headstone.

Reports of his activities from the *Northern Star* show that throughout his ten years with the National Charter Association and other associated organisations, he was well liked and respected for his impartiality.

This was a sad ending for one of the Chartists' relatively undistinguished but ardent supporters who had reached the peak of the Chartist Administration. However, he had lived to hear of the Reform League's success with the passing of the Second Reform Act that received Royal Assent in August, 1867. The Act extended the franchise that moved by further stages eventually to universal suffrage.

Two years after John Arnott's death, his wife, Sarah Arnott, died on the 17 February 1870 age 71 of 'Senile Decay'. She was still living at 1, Equity Buildings, Somers Town. The informant – who made her mark - was Eleanor Arnott, daughter-in-law, (wife of Arnott's son, Benjamin) of 41, Middlesex Street, Somers Town.

In his tour of the area, Charles Booth in 1898 wrote of Equity Buildings as a queer little paved cul-de-sac; low one storey two-roomed cottages, with a little wash house and yard behind; been done up during last year; doors open straight into room; many of the houses appeared to be very full of furniture; rents from 6/6 to 7/-.

Equity Buildings are marked on large scale maps of the period. Now redeveloped, it was between what is now Ossulston Street and Polygon Road, with the entrance in Phoenix Road. See the 1863 map as illustrated.

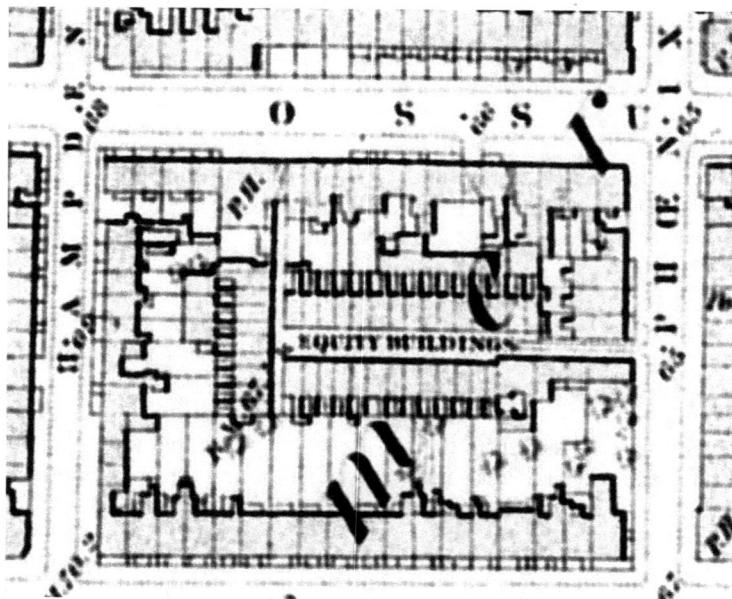

Equity Buildings, Somers Town

Of interest to Genealogists, I append details of a few of John Arnott's children:

1871 census.

No Arnotts listed at 41 Middlesex Street.
21 Middlesex Street, Alfred Arnott, 47, Shoemaker. Eliza Arnott (wife) 45. Charles, 21, Carman. Eliza, 15, Shop girl. Willie, 4.

*1, Phoenix Street, St Pancras. Edwin Arnott, brother, 30, Upholsterer.
Emma Arnott, sister, 34, Shoe-binder. Emily A., neice, 10.*
Phoenix Street was near Equity Buildings where Sarah Arnott died in
1870.

1881 census.

*6, New Street, Chelmsford (The King William the 4th Inn). Benjamin
Arnott, lodger, 51, Hawker. b. Chesham.*

*13 George Street, St Pancras. Edwin Arnott, 40, Upholsterer. Sarah
Arnott, wife, 41, b. Cleeve, Glos. Ben Etheridge, visitor, 7, b.
Mitcheldene, Glos.*

22 March 1890.
Eleanor Arnott, wife of Benjamin Arnott, Roadsman, died age 62 of
Acute Bronchitis at 29 Chalk Farm Road. Daughter, M. Arnott.

11 January 1908
Benjamin Arnott, 77, formerly a Hawker, of 43 Little George Street, St
Pancras, died of Bronchitis on 11 January 1908, at St Anne's House,
Streatham Hill.
St Anne's House was a branch of St Pancras Workhouse for some 500
aged and infirm men.

References:

A History of the Working Men's Association from 1836 to 1850.
George Howell, 1900. Frank Graham, Newcastle, 1970.
A Memoir of Thomas Martin Wheeler, by William Stevens.
John Bedford Leno, 1862.
Bishopsgate Library (Howell/11/2D/131) as cited.
Charles Booth's notes for his *Life and Labour of the People of London*,
a selection digitised – and online – by the London School of
Economics.
Illustrated London News, as cited.
Northern Star for the dates cited.
Ragged London in 1861, by John Hollingshead. Smith, Elder. Dent,
1986.
Somers Town. A Record of Change, by Malcolm Holmes.
London Borough of Camden, 1989.

St Pancras Workhouse Admissions Register, London Metropolitan
   Archives, ST/P/DG/160/001.
The Chartist Land Company, by A.M. Hadfield. David & Charles, 1970.
The National Charter Association and its role in the Chartist movement,
   1840 – 1858, by John Richard Clinton. M.Phil. thesis, Univ.
   Southampton, 1980.
   This is a useful work to use in conjunction with the main works on
   Chartism.
Times, as cited.

Further information of the period from Harney's *Red Republican* and
Friend of the People. But for a wider range of opinion, it is necessary to
consult the main published works on Chartism and other radical
newspapers of the time.

INDEX

John James Bezer		
Saturday	Equal	Strong Orbs
24/08/1816 11:30:00	Time Zone: 0:00W	Summer Time: 0:00
London	England	51N30 0W10

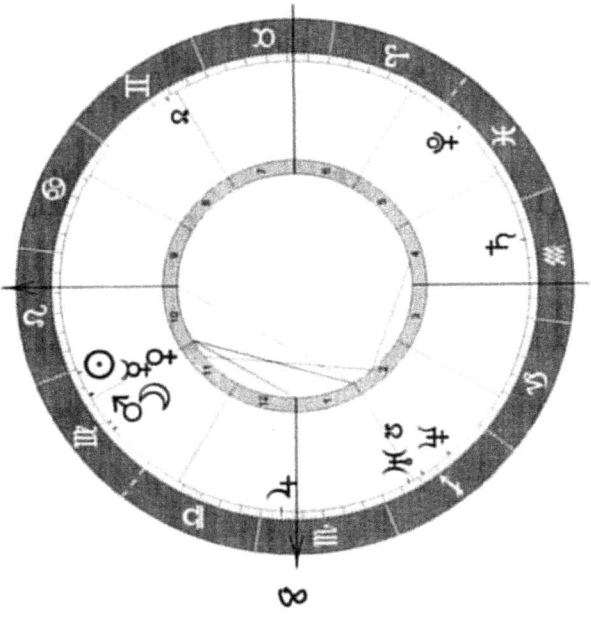

	Degree	Sign	House	Rx
☉	1.06	♍	10	
☽	17.48	♍	11	
☿	7.13	♍	10	
♀	7.36	♍	10	
♂	15.46	♍	11	
♃	4.52	♏	12	
♄	19.54	♒	4	Rx
♅	7.22	♐	1	
♆	19.22	♐	2	Rx
♇	23.32	♓	5	Rx
☊	11.18	♊	8	
☋	11.18	♐	2	

The above chart, inserted without comment, may be of interest to some readers. The time as given by Bezer in his autobiography is probably accurate to within ± 15 minutes.

www.ingramcontent.com/pod-product-compliance
Lightning Source LLC
La Vergne TN
LVHW050047090426
835511LV00033B/2377